Yasuhisa Miyake

Cognition, Macroeconomics and Economic Policy of Yamada Houkoku

University Education Press

Contents

Part I　Relevance, Cognition and Macroeconomic Policy:New interpretation on J. M. Keynes's general theory, new classical economics and economic policy of Yamada Houkoku 5

Preface　6
Foreword　9

Chapter1　The Tokugawa Bakufu and Economic Policy of
　　　　　Yamada Houkoku 15
　　1.1 Political and Economic Situations in the Tokugawa
　　　　period　15
　　1.2 The life and economic achievements of Yamada
　　　　Houkoku　18

Chapter2　Economic Policy and Economic Mind of Yamada
　　　　　Houkoku 27
　　2.1 Yamada Houkoku and the creation of government
　　　　enterprise　27

Chapter3　Macroeconomics and Cognition 33
　　3.1 Macroeconomics and cognitive linguistics　33
　　3.2 Economic principle in linguistics and cognition　38
　　3.3 Economic principle in economics and unemployment
　　　　　　　　　　　　　　　　　　　　　　　　44

Chapter4　Macroeconomics and Relevance 49
　　4.1 Macroeconomics and relevance theory　49

    4.2 Macroeconomics and some unpleasant rational
        expectations hypothesis　57
    4.3 Macroeconomics and liquidity trap　64

Postscript　72
Afterword　75

Part II　On the Economics of J. M. Keynes, New Classical Economics and Generative Economics:"A study in Relevance, Cognition and Macroeconomic Theory"...81

Preface　82
Foreword　85

Chapter1　A Critical View of General Theory.................92

Chapter2　J. M. Keynes's Treatise on Probability, New
            Classical Economics and Relevance Theory...99

Chapter3　Expectation and Relevance Theory 103

Chapter4　A Multiplier Effect and a Fractal-based
            Economic System..108

Chapter5　Generative Economics, Current Macroeconomics
            and Communication...................................121

Short notes on the real causes of economic depression　131
Supplement: a proposal for the establishment of
"International Buikukyoku"　134

Part I

Relevance, Cognition and Macroeconomic Policy:New interpretation on J. M. Keynes's general theory, new classical economics and economic policy of Yamada Houkoku

Preface
The economy : A World of Troubles

Peter Gunbel says in the Following way.

Political leaders will meet in London to try to rescue a global economy in its worst shape in decades. A look at how four countries are hurting. More than six months have passed since Lehman Brothers went bankrupt and Wall Street teetered on the edge of oblivion, but the bad news from the world of business and finance keeps on rolling. If anything, it's gotten worse. The financial mess still has not been cleaned up, on March 23, Treasury Secretary Tim Geithner presented yet another gazillion-dollar plan to detoxify the balance sheets of U.S. banks.

And around the world - from Raleigh N.C. to Riga, Latvia-every day brings fresh reports of gloom. The international Monetary Fund has predicted that for the first time in 60 years, world economic activity will decline in 2009.

You can quibble with the pessimism and reject the now commonplace comparisons with that other financial crash of the past century, that of 1929. But pick up the authoritative book on the earlier crisis by John Kenneth.

Galbraith and two chilling sentences leap out : "The singular feature of the Great Crash of 1929. "he wrote ,was that the worst continued to worsen. What looked one day like the end proved on the next day to have been only the beginning?"

It's against this bleak background that government leaders from the world's 20 major economics will gather in

London on April 2 in an attempt to come up with coordinated fixes for the two issues they all deem critical: how to prevent a recession from turning into a worldwide depression and how to restore confidence in financial markets. The auspices are not favorable, many countries have announced economic-stimulus packages, but national efforts have rarely been coordinated.(Peter Gumbel *Time* : April 6, 2009)

The financial and economic crash of 2008 led to economic recession which seemed to be more harmful than that of 1981-82. The financial crisis has deeply damaged consumers and business.

The problem is that monetary and fiscal policy is not effective with respect to output and employment, and people tend to spend less.

Conventional wisdom says that one of the reasons why the financial system collapsed is due to the collapse of housing prices and the subprime mortgage market.

If the market is anticipating an even worse drop in corporate profits and it is due to the fact that consumers spend less, the important point for economic recovery is that the market anticipates a better upturn in corporate profits and consumers spend much.

The basic way to revitalize an ailing economy is not to ease monetary policy and increase fiscal spending, but to convince the market that corporate profits must increase. The world is now finding the solution about how to prevent a world recession and restore confidence in financial markets.

I hope that this book contributes to prevent the current economic crisis from turning into protectionism, contraction of world trade and a great depression.

This book suggests that economic recovery consists in the creation of world trade based upon mutual advantage comparative advantage, specialization and exchange of goods.

Yasuhisa Miyake
August 2012

Foreword

I myself have taught philosophy and economic policy of Yamada Houkoku at Sanyo Gakuen University and am currently General-Secretary of Yamada Houkoku Research Association. I owe intellectual debts to Nihon University, Okayama University, Kyoto University, London University and Kwansei Gakuin University.

My intellectual thanks go to Mr. Tomoyoshi Ozaki, Ms. Kyoko Imamura, Professor Kenichi Ota, Professor Kazuo Yoshida, Professor Hiromi Yamamoto, Professor Fukuo Youichi, Professor Eiji Ouizumi, Professor Shigeru Sugitani, Professor Richard Portes, Professor David Begg, Professor Dennis Snower, Professor Ron Smith, Professor Elias Karakitsos, Professor Kiichi Masuhata, Professor Michio Hosaka.

My emotional thanks go to Toru Nojima, Minoru Hayase, Toshiaki Ousuga, Teruo Notohara, Junzo Yamashita, Chuji Sakamoto, and Kaname Asamori.

I have been greatly influenced by economics of Keynes.

John Maynard Keynes emphasizes economic concept of a liquidity trap in *The General Theory*, which means that people prefer holding cash to holding goods.

It seems that economics of Keynes put a great emphasis upon a psychological and cognitive factor. However, some western economics seem to put too much emphasis upon the theory of quantity or the theory of objectivity.

Yamada Houkoku was successful in changing people's attitudes that prefer holding cash to holding goods into the quite opposite attitudes. The reason is that his economic policy was based upon not only theory of quantity and the theory of objectivity, but also the theory of subjectivity and cognition. In other words, he made every effort to achieve lowering the value of holding cash and increasing the value of holding goods by changing people's perception upon currency.

I believe that economic mind of Yamada Houkoku will contribute to the development of economics of Keynes.

Unlike J. M. Keynes, economic policy of Yamada Houkoku tells us that a government should intervene in the market, creates a government enterprise which makes a complementary goods for a private enterprise and economic web based upon a complementary division of labor.

In other words, economic lessons for economic policy of Yamada Houkoku means that a complementary division of labor leads to the increase in employment and the expansion of market.

Unlike Adam Smith, Yamada Houkoku seems to emphasize that a complementary division of labor creates new market.

A complementary goods which a government enterprise creates adds value to a capitalist economy. A creation of a government enterprise implies that this leads to the increase in the profits of a private company. If Yamada Houkoku lived now. he would create a public employment company which solves the problem of a mismatch between employers and employees.

He would also create a public financial company which collects money and make investments to stabilize the financial market, and a public company which provides a business information.

For J. M. Keynes, public investment and public expenditure matter.

On the other hand, public investment and public expenditure do not matter for Yamada Houkoku. J. M. Keynes ignores the concept of emergence, complementary goods and the importance of DNA. What matters for Yamada Houkoku is economic DNA and a biological machine. If a dog, a cat and human beings eat quite the same food, they can't become the same thing. What makes them different is DNA. The creation of a government enterprise, new economic DNA does matter for economic recovery and economic prosperity, which purchases different goods, produces different goods and sells different goods, according to the change in demand and economic structure.

Economics of Adam Smith, Karl Marx, J. M. Keynes except Schumpeter ignores the importance of emergence. On the other hand, economics of Schumpeter ignores the role of government which creates "creative innovation". Yamada Houkoku would create "International Buikukyoku" which creates "creative innovation". This organization is not supposed to create "destructive innovation" and a huge public expenditure, which would lead to public debts Adam Smith is critical of. If a private enterprise behaves according to economic principle, this leads to unemployment. On the other hand, if a government enterprise behaves according to noneconomic principle this also leads to unemployment.

However, different economic goods of a government enterprise and a private enterprise create "creative innovation" and then this leads to employment and output.

Yamada Houkoku would say that the marginal propensity to consume or the multiplier effect is determined by economic web.

Unlike J. M. Keynes, Yamada Houkoku would say that what matters for economic prosperity is "information and knowledge" for effectual demand.

Unlike J. M. Keynes, who argues that the multiplier effect and the marginal propensity to consume determines national income, economic policy of Yamada Houkoku tells us that the multiplier effect and the marginal propensity to consume depend upon economic web and economic structure. If this is true, economic policy to achieve economic prosperity must be to create "new economic web" with current economic web. Discretionary fiscal policy and monetary policy may not be effective with respect to output and employment.

One of the real causes of economic depression is due to "current economic web itself". If this is true, a creation of "new economic web" would lead to economic recovery and the stability of financial market.

The above argument is very critical of a new classical economics that a government should intervene in the market to create new economic web. The number of purchase and selling increases as the extent and degree of economic depression decrease. If economy consists of only a private enterprise based upon a profit motive and economic principle, economic depression makes the number of them decrease indefinitely.

Thus, the solution for it is to create a government enterprise which is engaged in the purchase and selling of goods. Economic depression implies overproduction of goods.

If this is true public investments and public expenditure makes overproduction stronger.

If Yamada Houkoku lived now, he would lessen

overproduction.

Unlike J. M. Keynes, he would be critical of government expenditures based upon fiscal deficit to increase effective demand. Economics of J. M. Keynes and The General Theory ignores the interplay between yin and yang [1].

A healthy economy must consist in balancing yin and yang elements.

If we regard a private investment, a public investment, and overproduction as the bright yang, then a government intervention to increase effective demand implies a disruption of the balance of yin and yang. On the other hands, a government intervention to purchase economic goods from a private sector, when their prices are low, implies the balance of yin and yang.

Economic policy of Yamada Houkoku implies the action which is not contrary to nature.

Economic depression implies that a private firm wants to refrain from making investments and employment. The depressed prices implies that a private firm wants to sell his goods in order to increase his profits.

The general theory of J. M. Keynes implies the action which is contrary to nature (a private firm).

Unlike J. M. Keynes, the government intervention by Yamada Houkoku follows the nature of economic activities, a profit motive of human beings and an invisible hand. Therefore it does not take so much time for the economy to reach to the equilibrium.

Inflation target, money supply control and the government intervention to increase the depressed prices do not follow the nature of economic activities.

Note
(1)The Taoists saw all changes in nature as manifestations of the dynamic interplay between the polar opposites yin and yang, and thus they came to believe that any pair of opposites constitutes a polar relationship where each of the two polar is dynamically linked to the other.

For the western mind, this idea of the implicit unity of all opposites is extremely difficult to accept it.

It seems most paradoxical to us that experiences and values which we had always believed to be contrary should be, after all, aspects of the same thing.

Fritjof Carpra, *The Tao of physics an exploration of the parallels between modern physics and eastern mysticism*, Shambhala, 2000, pp.114-115.

Chapter 1
The Tokugawa Bakufu and Economic Policy of Yamada Houkoku

1.1 Political and Economic Situations in the Tokugawa period

The financial deficit of the Tokugawa Bakufu was financed not by issuing paper currency but by debasement of the coinage. Economic theory tells us that the cash expenditures based upon debasement of the coinage will lead to inflationary results. However, inflation did not occur and prices were stable because the increasing demand for cash matched the increasing demand for commercial transactions. The Tokugawa Bakufu depended on economic policy of price controls and had the great interest in maintaining and stabilizing the price of rice.

Economic policy of Tokugawa Bakufu was characterized by regulation and control, and the Bakufu did not rely on the operation of market forces.

In case that prices in Edo rose, the Bakufu ordered merchants to reduce commodities. If the price of rice fell in the market, because of crop failures, the Bakufu ordered the merchants to increase their stocks, and lend them money to buy them.

Under such a regulated economic system, the free market worked. This means that the Tokugawa economic system was not completely based upon the free market. All the domains were not allowed to issue coinage like silver coins or gold coins, and therefore they were obliged to issue paper currency, called "Hansatsu" if they were permitted to do so, by the Tokugawa Bakufu. Many domains were accumulating a mounting burden of debt because of for example, traveling costs to and from Edo, although they increased revenues by raising the rate of agricultural tax to cope with a mounting burden of debt, and increase their revenue.

They created monopoly marketing boards, called "Buikukyoku" whose purpose was to encourage production and processing of agricultural and industrial crops and shares in the profit from their production and sale through merchant. The Buikukyoku did not have the right to issue coinage in order to finance the purchase of economic goods and therefore, issued paper currency or paper notes, after getting the permission from the Bakufu.

It had placed strict controls and regulations on such issues. However, it was obliged to give many domains the right to issue them with the growth of local industry and commerce in the early years of the nineteenth century. Paper currency or paper notes issued by many domains were backed by coinage, rice, or goods. Paper currency called "Hansatsu" was in principle legally accepted within the domain. However, some "Hansatsu" gained acceptance beyond the borders. By the 1860s, the amount of such notes or papers increased greatly and they circulated and were exchanged with a large discount rate against coinage like silver coins or gold coins.

Some economists say that they were responsible for inflationary effects. However if the purpose of issuing such paper or notes was production-motive, not financing fiscal deficit, the economic effects of them might be tolerable and acceptable.

The Buikukyoku, a government bureau for savings and

investment, had been set up in the eighteenth century and the purpose was to invest in income-earning projects. The Buikukyoku had bought up the products not only of their own domains but of other domains, sending them to Osaka or Edo. It might contribute to curb merchant monopoly profits and lower prices. The Buikukyoku, the monopoly marketing board was linked with the issue of "Hansatsu", local paper currency. Local purchase were paid for in hansatsu and sales in the large cities like Osaka or Edo were for gold coins or silver coins. The Buikukyoku, based upon cooperation among producers, local merchants and domain governments, could be very successful. Faith in the "invisible hand" and the philosophy of laissez faire were unacceptable in the economy of Tokugawa era.

1.2 The life and economic achievements of Yamada Houkoku

Yamada Houkoku was born on Feb. 21 in Takahashi city of Okayama prefecture(Present) in 1805. In 1860,he was appointed as finance minister of Bitchu Matsuyama Han (a domain government). Yamada's successful career started in Bittyu Matsuyama Han, where he made great contributions to education, military security, social welfare and economic development. He worked out his philosophy of mercy for poor farmers. Faced with financial crisis and economic depression and accumulated debts, he carried out revolutionary economic reforms. Yabuki Kunihiko describes Yamada Houkoku as an early Keynesian, probably because, during his years, fiscal spending rose and Houkoku government's production to accelerate industrialization might had combined with steps to spur private production.

Houkoku policies were characterized by not only higher fiscal spending for public infrastructure but also fiscal austerity such as reduction in wages and salaries for high ranking officials, not lowest officials and therefore, he may be described as one of early Adam Smith-type economists. Houkoku has become known for political and economic reforms such as maximizing exports to Edo. Faced with crop failures that might lead to serious famine, he invested major resources for poor farmers, and therefore peasant rebellions and protests never occurred. Although Yamada Houkoku's period of influence was actually short, he began with measures to curb the corruption and assentation.

Houkoku, influenced by Confucianism, was particularly intent on ways to tidy up educational and intellectual scene. He set up a school to which he admitted students from all social classes, including peasant class. He was a moral, conscientious administrator. His intelligence, honesty, academic learning, and a vigorous purge won him esteem, especially among peasant class.

He followed not only Chu Xi Confucianism, but also another Confucianism who asserted that thought and action were inseparable. Unlike Houkoku, arrogant bureaucrats were indifferent to the misery of the people who suffered from crop failures, which often caused peasant protest occur. [1] He restored the moral government and saved the people. Economic reforms became a matter of urgency for most domains, because financial debts continued to grow large, and therefore there was not any domain which has not borrowed from the rich merchants. In other words, Domain governments and administrators were obliged to borrow money from them for interests payments. The alternative solution was that they tried to get more out of their people. In other words, they tried to increase the taxes borne by its farmers.

It was obvious that the possibility of the risks of protest increased as the rate of taxes continued to rise. The other alternative solution was their announcement of cancellation of debts to their own merchants or renegotiation on better terms. If the domain proposed renegotiating its debts with his creditors over more than 100-year period, this would mean his declaration of bankruptcy. On the other hand, Houkoku did not announce his cancellation of debts to his own merchants, although he renegotiated with his creditors on better terms. He also did not try to get more out of his people, especially poor peasants or low ranking officials.

He set up a government bureau for savings and

investment, called " the Buikukyoku", and it was directed to investment in income-earning projects.

Merchant's monopolies and internal commerce had suppressed producer prices in order to maximize their profits. With a free market whose producer prices were based upon demand and supply, however, they might had continued to rise.

Houkoku's campaign against their monopolies, ironically led to the creation of "the Buikukyoku" based upon his monopoly and the dissolution of merchant monopolies. It continued to buy up the products from its own domain and sent them to other domains when the market price was high. He tried to curb merchant profits and increase his people's real purchasing power.

Economic logic tells us that a domain government effort to increase his income creates a conflict with Bakufu income. However, Houkoku's effort to increase Bitchu Matsuyama income contributed to economic development of Edo (present-day, Tokyo), because his trading system with Edo was based upon comparative advantage. For example, " Bitchu Guwa(備中鍬)" whose purpose was to increase the amount of agricultural products was made from iron and coal.

Bitchu Matsuyama domain was rich in iron and coal, and Edo was not rich in iron and coal. The "Buikukyoku" lent money to his people and recommended them to make " Bitchu Guwa". The making of them was conditional upon the fact that it promised to buy them back. In other words, capitalist economy was based upon uncertainty and Bitchu Matsuyama economy was based upon certainty, In the capitalist economy with financial crisis and great depression, the increase in money supply does not remove liquidity trap. However, in the Bitchu Matsuyama economy, the increase in money supply does remove liquidity trap. " Bitchu Guwa" was sent to Edo and it contributed to the increase in agricultural products like rice in Edo. In other words, "Buikukyoku" in Bitchu Matsuyama Han creates "creative creation" not destructive creation among Bittyu Matsuyama's financial position, his people and Edo economy. In other words, Houkoku makes Bitchu Matsuyama Han, his people and people in Edo happy at the same time.

Money supply from "Buikukyoku" creates effective demand, increase productivity between Bitchu Matsuyama economy and Edo economy, and stabilizes product prices. Money creation contributes to the reduction in Bitchu Matsuyama's fiscal debts because "Buikukyoku" creates huge profits for Bictyu Matsuyama's economy.

Before Houkoku was appointed as finance minister of Bittyu Matsuyama, the Bitchu Matsuyama's paper currency, called "Hansatsu" was depreciating against gold or silver coins. In other words, his people tried to exchange "Hansatsu" with gold coins or silver coins as soon as possible. The number of people who tried to exchange "Hansatsu" with specie reserves continued to increase as the value of it continued to go down.

This depreciated paper currency might have caused a hyperinflation in Bitchu Matsuyama domain because people preferred commodities which were stable in value to the depreciating paper currency.

Ben S. Bernanke says in the following way.

> the idea of debt-deflation goes back to Irving Fisher (1933).

Fisher envisioned a dynamic process in which falling asset and commodity prices created pressure on nominal debtors, forcing them into distress sales of assets, which in turn led to further price declines and financial difficulties. His diagnosis led him to urge President Roosevelt to subordinate exchange-rate considerations to the need for reflation, advice that (ultimately) FDR followed Fisher's idea was less influential in academic circles, though, because of the counterargument that debt-deflation represented no more than a redistribution from one group (debtors) to another (creditors).Absent implausibly large differences in marginal spending propensities among the groups, it was suggested pure redistributions should have no significant macroeconomic effects. However, the debt-deflation idea has recently experienced a revival which has drawn its inspiration from the burgeoning literature on imperfect information and agency costs in capital markets.

According to the agency approach, which has come to dominate modern corporate finance, the structure of balance sheets provides an important mechanism for aligning the incentives of the borrower (the agent) and the lender (the principal). One central feature of the balance sheet is the borrower's net worth, defined to be the borrower's own ("internal") funds plus the collateral value of his illiquid assets. Many simple principal-agent models imply that a decline in the borrower's net worth increases the deadweight agency cost of lending and thus the net cost of financing the borrower's proposed investments. Intuitively, if a borrower can contribute relatively little to his or her own project and hence most rely primarily on external finance, then the borrower's incentives to take actions that are not in the lender's interest may be relatively high, the result is both deadweight losses (for example, inefficiently high risk-taking or low effort) and the necessity of costly information provision and monitoring. If the borrower's net worth falls below a threshold level, he or she may not be able to obtain funds at all.

From the agency perspective, a debt-deflation that unexpectedly redistributes wealth away from borrowers is not a macroeconomically neutral event. To the extent that potential borrowers have unique or lower-cost access to particular investment projects or spending opportunities, the loss of borrower net worth effectively cuts off these opportunities from the economy. Thus, for example, a financially distressed firm may not be able to obtain working capital necessary to expand production, or to fund a project that would be viable under better financial conditions. Similarly, a house-hold whose current nominal income has fallen relative to its debts may be barred from purchasing a new home, even though purchase is justified in a permanent-income sense. By inducing financial distress in borrower firms and households, debt-deflation can have real effects on the economy. [2]

On the other hand, the debt-deflation idea was adequate and obvious for explaining Bitchu Matsuyama Han's economy.

The depreciated value in Hansatsu led to the reduction of his people's purchasing power, economic depression and fiscal deficit.

Yamada Houkoku promised to exchange the depreciated paper currency with silver coins. Specie reserves were based upon the Buikukyoku's profits or borrowing from merchants in Osaka or Edo. Houkoku burned the collected Hansatsu in front of his people and spent many hours in burning them in order to make them know that they were burned, money supply was reduced and the ratio between Hansatsu and reserves changed.

Then, he issued the new paper currency called "Eisen(永銭)", which was guaranteed to exchange with gold coins, not silver coins whose value was appreciating against silver coins. Gold coins reserves was based upon the profits from Edo. In Edo, the key currency for economic transaction was gold coins and silver coins were the key currency in Bittyu Matsuyama domain. He lent his people the new paper currency and recommended them to produce economic goods which were promised to be bought back by the domain. It was a logical conclusion that they were happy to accept it.

It might be considered that if his people accept new hansatsu and never exchange it with gold coins whose value is increasing, he does not need to increase the amount of gold coins reserves even if the amount of paper currency in circulation increases. In other words, he could have taken advantage of this reserves for speculation and made huge profits by making use of price fluctuation such as rice, silver coins, gold coins and commodities.

It might be considered that if he purchases economic goods from his people at a higher price, then their income and real purchasing power increases and therefore economic recovery comes back to normal.

His domain might have made huge profits, although he purchased economic goods from his people at a higher price. The reason is as follows. He sent them to Edo, the capital of

Japan in Tokugawa period whose price of economic goods was the highest in Japan. This means that he took advantage of price differential between Bitchu Matsuyama Han and Edo.

As we mentioned earlier, Yamada Houkoku promised to exchange the depreciating paper currency called "Hansatsu" with silver coins and then issued the new paper currency. It was promised to exchange with gold coins whose value is appreciating against silver coins. New "Hansatsu" gained credit and was used for commercial transactions. The reason for the credibility was that it was connected with his domain's business activities (Buikukyoku). He was successful in changing the depreciating currency into the appreciating one without the huge amount of specie reserves or fiscal expenditures.

If we analyze his economic policy, his success might be based upon the fact that each economic policy he created was relevant.

Faced with the depreciating currency, he increased the amount of reserves, exchanged it with silver coins and issued new paper currency which was connected with his domain's business activities.

He seems to recognize the importance of his people's assumption, imagination and relevance between each economic policy. He tried to make his people assume that new paper currency would be accepted by other people.

What his economic policy contributes to modern economics is that relevance makes a central role in the stability of financial assets. Another contribution is that the establishment of government enterprise and the increase in his people's real purchasing power makes a central role in the recovery from great depression or financial crisis.

He exchanges the depreciating old currency with new paper currency and the point is that faced with the depreciating old currency against new paper currency, he made the exchange rate of old paper currency against new paper currency higher and therefore his people's real purchasing power and his people's income increases.

Note

(1) Economic theory Houkoku had in mind was that the government could not prosper unless the people, especially the poor peasants were prosperous. Therefore, economic policy to encourage production only for the government was against the theory.
(2) Ben S. Bernanke, *Essays on The Great Depression,*
    Princeton University Press, 2000, pp.24-25.

Chapter 2
Economic Dolicy and Economic Mind of Yamada Houkoku

2.1 Yamada Houkoku and the creation of government enterprise

If we define new economics based upon economic mind of Yamada Houkoku as Houkokunomics, "Houkokunomics" makes a proposal to create the Buikukyoku, a government bureau for savings and investment based upon a fractal-based economic system to correct loss of exchange of goods in the market and reduction in people's purchasing power. according to his economic policy, the purpose of government intervention and control of economy is to revitalize market mechanism. A fractal-based economic system must be connected with the division of labour. It can be explained in the following way.

The buikukyoku creates the situation whose economic diversity of goods creates economic diversity, employs involuntary unemployment and purchases economic goods and services from private enterprise.

It assumes that collapse of bubble and reduction in people's purchasing power make people spend less and therefore the efficient market for exchange of goods does not hold.

According to his economic policy, revitalizing barter economy means stimulating economy and money economy is one of the causes of economic depression. The Bitchu Matsuyama domain's economy was a fractal-based economic system and could be explained in the following way.

Its fractal-based economic system was connected with the division of labour. This means that farmers concentrate upon only making agricultural products and merchants concentrate upon only making a sales promotion.

What we should learn from Yamada Houkoku is that faced with economic depression, exchange of goods created by government and to revitalize the invisible hand through the creation of government enterprise is effective for economic recovery. According to his economic policy, the multiplier effect of fiscal spending that Buikukyoku purchases goods from private sector, depends upon the amount of economic network, not marginal propensity to consume[fig.1].

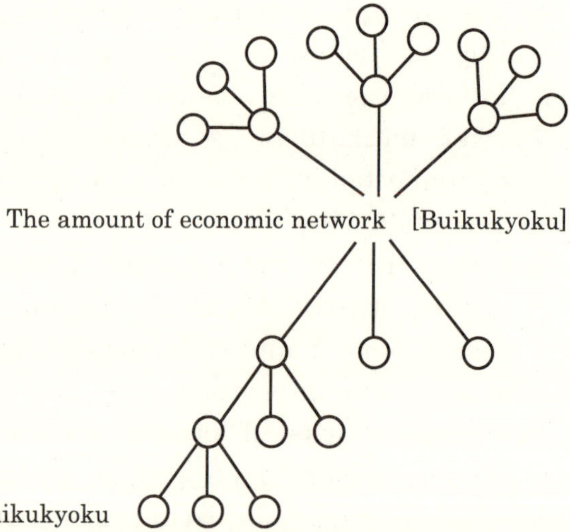

The amount of economic network   [Buikukyoku]

fig.1 Buikukyoku

If money economy is one of the causes of economic depression, it assumes that economic depression can not be solved only by money creation and fiscal expenditure.

Faced with liquidity trap, it unlike economics of Keynes, suggests that government stimulate and revitalize "barter economy", the flow of economic goods and creates the buikukyoku, the government enterprise.

It also suggests that government enterprise in each country cooperates to purchase economic goods from private enterprise and exchange them for each other at the same time. If the international cooperation based upon government enterprise is established, it may create the benevolent invisible hand, Adam Smith's central economic concept and prevent the liquidity trap, John Maynard Keynes's central economic concept.

If the creation of international central bank is needed, it is expected to have the legal right to issue yen, dollar, pound, other currencies, and international currency and lend them to central banks which lend them to government enterprise which purchase economic goods from private enterprise, and play the role in exchanging information among government enterprises.

The collapse of bubble and financial crisis leads to the fact that people spend less and the amount of consumption decreases. However, before and after the collapse of bubble and financial crisis, labour force, the supply of economic goods and services and technology remain constant. Only the value of money changes and it destroys the link between goods and money. If this is true, government must make a recovery for the link by creating the international Buikukyoku.

Economics of Adam Smith recognizes the importance of market for exchange but ignores the fact that fluctuations in the international financial market affects the efficient market for goods. On the other hand, Economics of John Maynard Keynes recognizes the effect of financial market upon real economy, but ignores the importance of the market for exchange for economic recovery.

Economic policy of Yamada Houkoku recognizes both the effect of financial market upon real economy and the importance of the market for exchange.

Direct approach of economic policy says that financial depression must be solved by the increase in money supply and fiscal expenditures. Indirect approach of economic policy says that financial depression must be solved by the increase in the flow and exchange of goods.

Economics of Keynes belongs to direct approach of economic policy and economic policy of Yamada Houkoku belongs to indirect approach of.[1]

It says that financial depression means the weakness of flow and exchange of goods and therefore, making the flow and exchange of goods stronger makes the power of the money stronger. In other words, it says that the depressed supply of goods means the weakness of power of money.

What it suggests is that money and goods are relative. In developing countries, financial assistance, government expenditures and public investment are important for the supply of goods. However, in developed countries like Japan, USA, England and Germany, financial assistance, government expenditure, public investment is not important for economic recovery from financial depression and the increase in money supply.

In the Tokugawa period which had money economy and developed economy, Yamada Houkoku created the buikukyoku, a government bureau to stimulate flow and exchange of goods.

The important thing for us to do now, faced with great depression and financial crisis, is to revitalize the exchange of abundant economic goods and services, labour force among local regions, large cities and countries.

It assumes that price fluctuations in the market are caused by a mismatch between demand and supply in time and place and the mismatch is one of the causes of economic depression.

It also assumes that, the persistence of economic depression is caused by collapse of bubble and reduction in people's purchasing power of money. In other words, money economy itself is the reason why great depression and financial crisis occurs. And therefore, the increase in people's purchasing power might be the key for economic recovery. However, Houkokunomics assumes that it might be a necessary condition for economic recovery and it might not be a sufficient condition.

Even if government increases money supply and fiscal spending, economy might not come back to normal without correcting a mismatch between demand and supply. If government provides the market for exchange of goods and stimulate an invisible demand, not effective demand, and makes private enterprises know what an invisible demand is(what people really want to get),economy might recover soon.

Collapse of bubble and financial crisis might disturb the smooth flow of economic goods and therefore, an invisible hand might not work. John Maynard Keynes emphasizes the importance of government intervention and stimulating effective demand.

On the other hand, Yamada Houkoku might emphasize the stability of currency, revitalize the efficient market for exchange of goods and create economic goods which is consistent with an invisible hand.

Notes
(1) Fritjof Capra says in the following way.
>the movements of the Tao are a continuous interplay between opposites, the Taoists deduced two basic rules for human conduct. Whenever you want to achieve anything, they said, you should start with its opposite, thus Lao Zi(老子), in order to weaken, one will surely strengthen first: in order to overthrow, one will surely exit first: in order to take, one will surely give first, this is called subtle wisdom. On the other hand, whenever you want to retain anything, you should admit in it something of its opposite: Be bent, and you will remain straight. Be vacant, and you will remain full. Be worn, and you will remain new.
>
>This is the way of life of the sage who has reached a higher point of view, a perspective from which the relativity and polar relationship of all opposites are clearly perceived. These opposites include, first and foremost, the concepts of good and bad which are interrelated in the same as yin and yang. Those who follow the natural order flow in the current of the Tao, 'non-action' refraining from activity contrary to nature. Non-action does not mean doing nothing and keeping silent.
>
>Let everything be allowed to do what it naturally does, so that its nature win be satisfied. If one refrains from acting contrary to nature or, as Needham says, from going against the grain of things, one is in harmony with the Tao and thus one's actions will be successful.
>
>The notion that all opposites are polar that light and dark, winning and losing, good and evil, are merely different aspects of the same phenomenon is one of the basic principles of the Eastern way of life. Since all opposites are interdependent their conflict can never result in the total victory of one side, but will always be a manifestation of the interplay between the two sides. The dynamic unity of polar opposites can be illustrated with the simple example of a circular motion and its projection.
>
>Suppose you have a ball going round a circle. If this movement is projected on to a screen, it becomes an oscillation between two extreme points. The ball goes round the circle with constant speed, but in the projection it slows down, as it reaches the edge, turn around, and then accelerates again only to slow down once more.

See, Fritof Capra, "The Tao of physics an exploration of the parallels between modern physics and Eastern mysticism", pp.114-118.
 The above argument says that the essence of economic lessons of

Houkoku is to follow natural order and indirect approach.

Chapter 3
Macroeconomics and Cognition

3.1 Macroeconomics and cognitive linguistics

Cognitive linguistics is a new theory of language that challenges the theory of generative grammar, developed by Noam Chomsky. Its focus on meaning is based upon the assumption that meaning is not independent of human perceptions and human cognition.

Cognitive linguistics tries to clarify the relationship between language and perspective to prove that linguistic expressions are reflections of a particular way of perceiving the world. It covers the nature of categories, constructional meaning, reference and may provide new approach for solving economic problems such as great depression or financial crisis.

Cognitive linguistics focus on the notions of construal, perspective, foregrounding, metaphor, and frame Cognitive linguistics is different from the theory of generative grammar, developed by Noam Chomsky in the sense that the former considers linguistic structure to be a direct reflex of cognition and the latter considers linguistic structure to be one determined by a formal rule system.

In other words, cognitive linguistics argues that a particular linguistic structure emerges out of a particular way of conceptualizing a given situation.

Unlike generative grammar which is based upon a set of

principles of language design that are specific to language, cognitive linguistics is based upon human cognition. [1]

Cognitive linguistics can be explained in the following way.

(1) John gave the book to Mary.
(2) John gave Mary the book.

Sentence (1) and Sentence (2) involve different ways of construing the same situation and the same situation is constituted by different conceptualizations.

(3) The path falls steeply into the valley.
(4) The path climbs steeply out of the valley.

sentence (3) and sentence (4) involve different perspectives of construing the same situation. sentence (3) is based upon the view that some looks down into the valley. On the other hand, sentence (4) is based upon the view that someone looks up from the valley floor. sentence (3) and sentence (4) involve contrasting perspectives and therefore produce distinct interpretations. Similar examples can be found in the following sentence.

(5) John bought the car from Mary.
(6) Mary sold the car to John.
(7) John bought the car from Mary for a good price.
(8) Mary sold the car to John for a good price.
(9) The lamp is above table.
(10) The table is below the lamp.[2]

The concept of metaphor is closely related with a very important feature of cognitive linguistics.

Lakoff and Johnson say that metaphor is a fundamental property of language. Metaphor is the notion that different ways of thinking about a particular phenomenon are associated with different metaphors.[3]

The concept of frame is closely related with a very important feature of cognitive linguistics. For example, a native speaker of English has a kind of frame about the word, wicket, but a non-native speaker of English do not have any kind of frame about it and therefore he must consult a dictionary for help.

The concept of frame tells us that a particular word is associated with a particular concept and different people have different concept. A particular word tends to make people to activate certain areas of their knowledge base, depending upon different degrees in different contexts.[4]

What cognitive linguistics contributes to economic policy is that the concepts such as perspective, frame, and metaphor is closely related with a particular imaging, people's knowledge base, and their process of interpretation about the situations.

If economic policy-makers change people's knowledge base, perspective, frame, metaphor etc, and then their process of interpretation about economic situations must change. Whether discretionary macro-economic policy is effective or not may depend upon people's schema, and frame of reference if the argument of cognitive linguistics is true.

If we combine economic mind of Yamada Houkoku with the concept of linguistics such as relevance theory and cognitive linguistics, and define it as Houkokunomics, Houkokunomics is different from Keynes's economics and new classical economics in the sense that discretionary macroeconomic policy may not be effective in one situation and it may be effective in another situation.

Faced with liquidity trap, economists who believe in the general theory may emphasize the importance of fiscal policy, not monetary policy. On the other hand, new classical economists may argue that discretionary macroeconomic policy is not effective if people are rational. Houkokunomics argues that whether discretionary macroeconomic policy is effective or not depends upon people's concept or image about fiscal policy, monetary policy, and government intervention in the forex market.

Goodhart's Law says that any observed statistical regularity will tend to collapse once pressure is placed upon it for control purposes.[5]

This means that any attempt by a government to control an economic variable is not effective, because people become aware of the government's attempt to control an economic variable and therefore this will distort the government plans. Goodhart's Law, the Lucas Critique, the Heisenberg Uncertainty Principle or quantum physics and the theory of dynamic inconsistency may emphasize the ineffectiveness of discretionary macroeconomic policy.

Economic policy of Yamada Houkoku may be inconsistent with Goodhart's Law. However, it is not inconsistent with Goodhart's Law, because economic policy of Yamada Houkoku supports self-interest of people, creates an invisible hand in the market, and therefore people behave the way Government expects to do.

Notes
(1) See David Lee, *Cognitive Linguistics an introduction,* Oxford university Press, 2001, p1.
(2) See David Lee, pp.2-4.
(3) See George Lakoff, and Mark Johnson, *Metaphors We Live By,* University of Chicago Press, 1980.
(4) See George Lakoff *Women, Fire and Dangerous things : What categories reveal about the mind,* University of Chicago Press, 1987.

The concept of metaphor can be explained in the following way.

"Eco (1984, 987) insists that metaphor defines every encyclopedic entry. Nevertheless, metaphor merits such an entry because, although sometimes seen as merely one among the different tropes (see Stylistics) available to a language user, it may equally be seen as a fundamental principle of all language use. It has even been claimed (Lakoff and Johnson, 1980, p.3) that our ordinary conceptual system, in terms of which we both think and act, is fundamentally metaphorical in nature. It should be pointed out, however, that even researchers taking a view of metaphor very much opposed to this would agree about the importance to linguistic theory of phenomenon of metaphor. Thus Sadock (1979), according to whom metaphor falls outside linguistics proper because it has nonlinguistic parallels while linguistics should be confined to the study of the uniquely linguistic aspects of human communication (p.46), believes, in spite of this, that an understanding of metaphor is important for linguists because figurative language is one of the most productive sources of linguistic change and most lexical items (are) dead metaphors (p.48).

Lakoff and Johnson's book presents the most extreme form of constructivism, one of the two broad categories into which theories of metaphor may fall the other being non-constructivism (Ortony, 1979, p.2). According to constructivism, the objective world is not directly accessible, but is constructed on the basis of the constraining influences of human knowledge and language.

On this view, metaphor may be seen as instrumental in creating reality, and the distinction between literal and figurative, including metaphorical, language tends to break down." (Kristen Malmkjaer (ed.) *Metaphor, The Linguistics Encyclopedia, edited by Kirsten Malmkjaer*, pp.308-309)

If we apply the theory of metaphor which means that the objective world is constructed on the basis of the constraining influences of human knowledge, to economic analysis, the effect of fiscal policy, monetary policy and government intervention in the forex market may be determined by the constraining influences of human knowledge about economics.

(5) C.A.E. Goodhart *Money, Information and Uncertainty*, Macmillan 1989.

3.2 Economic principle in linguistics and cognition

Noam Chomsky argues that principle of economy is relevant not only for the form and representation of structures but also for the processes that produce them.[1] In other words, language tends to use the minimum number of steps or processes and the principle of economy is closely related with minimalism with some quite the smallest possible set of devices. This means that minimalism requires that movement be over the shortest possible distance. Short moves are more economical than longer ones and the principle of economy requires that the linguistic system needs to be as economical as possible.[2] On the other hand, the principle of economy can be found in the literature of cognitive grammar. In human communication shared presuppositions encourage economical communication

However, politeness phenomena go in the opposite direction.
(1) Could you give me a sheet of paper?
(2) Give me a sheet of paper.

If we compare sentence (1) and sentence (2) sentence (2) is more economical than sentence (1). However sentence (1) is more polite than sentence (2). This means that there is a trade-off relationship between economy and politeness. In other words, as sentence or utterance departs from the principle of maximal economy of utterance, politeness increases.[3]

If we think of the reason why the principle of economy exists in human communication, the reason might be related with the limits of capacity of cognition.

Ulic Neisser says in the following way.

It is often argued that there must be an overall limit to a person's capacity for information. Acceptance of this assumption frequently goes along with some form of filter theory: a special mechanism is postulated to protect the limited capacity from overload. Arguments of this kind are common not only in experimental psychology but in neighboring disciplines. They have led neurophysiologists to look for filtering mechanisms in the nervous system and sociologists to bewail the information overload that burdens the inhabitants of modern society.

We have seen, however, that such filters are not needed and probably do not exist. In my opinion, the notion of a single central information limit is equally misguided. Human abilities do have limitations, but they are not so monolithic or quantitative as such a notion would suggest.

The very concept of 'capacity' seems better suited to a passive vessel into which things are put than to an active and developing structure. The belief in a fixed cognitive capacity has been so widely accepted that it deserves very careful examination. It has several roots.

One of them is closely related to the concept of consciousness, and will be considered in a later section of this chapter. Another, which can be quickly dismissed, is based on what appears to be a logical and a priori argument.

According to a theorem in the mathematical theory of communication, when the rate of information input to any finite channel exceeds a certain value (called the channel's capacity) not all of it can be transmitted without error. Because the brain itself is finite and because it transmits information, this theorem has been taken as proof that there must be a limit to human capacity as well.

> While such an argument is valid in principle, it is of dubious relevance to psychology.
>
> The brain contains millions of neurons in unimaginably subtle relationships with one another. Who can say how high the limit imposed by such a "mechanism" may be?
>
> No one has ever demonstrated that the facts of selective attention have any relation to the brain's real capacity, if it has one at all.[4]

This means that there is the inherent a symmetry between a perceiving individual and the entity perceived.[5] In other words, people tend to concentrate upon only a particular phenomenon of the situations and ignore other sides of them.

The above argument may be supported by the following argument. R. W. Langacker says in the following way.

> Mental experience is the flow of cognitive events. Conscious experience proceeds concurrently in numerous domains. The reality and importance of attention as a mental phenomenon are beyond dispute.
>
> Agreement is also easily reached on certain aspects of a phenomenological account of attention: it shifts quite readily from one domain to another and from one entity to another within a domain, to some extent, it is subject to volitional control (hence we can direct our attention or concentrate on something). And it lends itself, on introspective grounds, a sufficient frame of reference.[6]

If the above argument is true, human cognition based upon economic principle tends to vary over time.

Geoffrey N. Leech explains the economy principle in the following way.

> The Economy Principle (Be quick and easy) can be regarded as a valuable precept not only for h but for s. If one can shorten the text while will probably be preferred: (8a) James likes Mary more than Doris likes Mary. (8b) James likes Mary more than Doris does. (8c) James likes Mary more than Doris. The pragmatic point about reduction is that it abbreviates the text, and often simplifies its structure, while maintaining the recoverability of the message.
>
> It is when, for some reason, the message's recoverability is impaired that reduction comes into conflict with the Clarity Principle keeping the message unimpaired, this reduces the amount of time and effort involved both in encoding and in decoding. As this description implies, the Economy Principle is continually at war with the Clarity Principle. On the phonological level for example, economy favors elisions, assimilations, and other abbreviating and simplifying processes. But obviously to maximize the principle of least effort in this way would be to make the text unintelligible. In practice, a balance has to be struck between saving time and effort, and maintaining intelligibility. This balance will clearly depend in part on contextual factors, such as the physical distance between s and h, and the social predictability of the message.
>
> Similarly, on the syntactic level, the Economy Principle has a contributory maxim of reduction which might be simply enunciated as reduce where possible. But reduction should evidently not be recommended where it leads to ambiguity. The processes which are subsumed under the

heading of 'reduction' here are (a) pronominalization (b) substitution by other pro-forms, e.g.: do so and (4). If the baby won't drink cold milk, it should be boiled. (c) ellipsis (or deletion). For example, sentence (4) above is an example of injudicious pronominalization: in order to avoid ambiguity in this case, s would have to sacrifice economy by repeating the noun milk. (b) If the baby won't drink cold milk, the milk should be boiled.

The same considerations apply to other forms of reduction, for example, to pro-form substitution and ellipsis: (7a) James enjoys golf more than James enjoys tennis. (7b) James enjoys golf more than he does tennis. (7c) James enjoys golf more than tennis of (7a) - (7c), the longest sentence, (7a) is the 'unhappiest' variant and the shortest one (7c) is the 'happiest'.

Thus for the Principle of Economy dictates the preferences. But if the most reduced form, as in (8c) below, introduces ambiguity, then a less reduced but unambiguous sentence, e.g. (8b).[7]

Notes
(1) See Vivian Cook and Mark Newson, *Chomsky's universal Grammar*, Blackwell, 1996, pp.168-169.
(2) See Vivian Cook and Mark Newson, p312, p337.
(3) See Peter Grundy, *Doing Pragmatics Amold*, 1995, p.69, p.128.
(4) See Ulric Neisser, *Cognition and Reality principles and implications of cognitive psychology*, W. H. Freeman and company 1976, pp.97-98.
(5) Ronald W. Langacker says that the contrast between subjective and objective construal therefore reflects the inherent asymmetry between a perceiving individual and the entity perceived. The asymmetry is maximized when the perceiver is so absorbed in the perceptual experience that he loses all awareness of self; and when the object perceived is well-delimited, wholly distinct from the perceiver, and located in a region of high perceptual acuity.
Cognitive Linguistics Research, Concept, Image and Symbol : the

cognitive basis of grammar Ronald W. Langacker, Mouton De Gruyter 1990, p316.
(6) See Ronald W. Langacker
Foundations of cognitive grammar, volume I, theoretical prerequisites, Stanford University Press, 1987, pp.114-115.
(7) Geoffrey N. Leech, *Principles of Pragmatics,* Longman, 1983.

3.3 Economic principle in economics and unemployment

If causes of unemployment are the fact that economic principle dominates and controls the behavior of capitalists or entrepreneurs, fiscal policy or monetary policy is ineffective with respect to output or employment. Concept of economic principle can be found in Marx's "Capital, General Theory and Wealth of Nations. "

If we define economic principle as maximizing profits and minimizing costs, capitalists or entrepreneurs tend to reduce employment costs even in normal times.

As we mentioned earlier, concept of economic principle can be found in linguistics literature. For example, the economy principle holds that the shortest grammar is the best grammar and human communication based upon only economic principle loses politeness. The same logic could be applied to economic phenomena. In other words, business activities based upon only economic principle tend to cause economic depression which leads to a high rate of unemployment. As J. M. Keynes mentions in "The General Theory", the marginal efficiency of capital represents economic principle.

As long as capitalists maximize the difference between the prospective yield of a capital-asset and its supply price or replacement cost, economic recession is inevitable.

J. M. Keynes says in the following way.

> The excess of the value of the resulting output over the sum of its factor cost and its user cost is the profit or the income of the entrepreneur.
>
> Thus the factor cost and the entrepreneur's profit make up,

between them, what we shall define as the total income resulting from the employment given by the entrepreneur. The entrepreneur's profit thus defined is as it should be. The quantity which he endeavors to maximize when he is deciding what amount of employment to offer for entrepreneurs will endeavor to fix the amount of employment at the level which they expect to maximize the excess of the proceeds over the factor cost. The volume of employment is given by the point of intersection between the aggregate demand function and the aggregate supply function, for it is at this point that the entrepreneurs' expectation of profits win be maximized.[1]

However, Houkokunomics criticizes Keynes's argument, because the firm's behavior based upon economic principle does not determine the volume of employment at the level of intersection between the aggregate demand function and the aggregate supply, because entrepreneurs will endeavor to fix the amount of employment at the level which they expect to maximize profits and minimize costs.

As long as they maximize profits by minimizing costs, increasing effective demand does not lead to the increase in employment. In addition to capitalists or entrepreneurs, people make economic situations worse by maximizing their profits and minimizing their costs. For example, liquidity preference is the obvious economic phenomenon, which people prefer cash to holding a debt which produce a very low rate of interest.

Karl Marx's "Capital" tells us that capitalist economy is inherently unstable and tends to produce involuntary unemployment, because of economic principle of capitalists.

Karl Marx says in the following way.

The mass of the means of production which he thus transforms, increases with the productiveness of his labour. But those means of production play a double part. The increase of some is a consequence, that of the others a condition of the increasing productivity of labor. E.g. with the division of labor in manufacture, and with the use of machinery, more raw material is worked up in the same time, and therefore, a greater mass of raw material and auxiliary substances enter into the labour-process. That is the consequence of the increasing productivity of labour.

On the other hand, the mass of machinery, beasts of burden, mineral manures, drain-pipes & C is a condition of the increasing productivity of labour. So also is it with the means of production concentrated in buildings, furnaces, means of transport & C. But whether condition or consequence, the growing extent of the means of production, as compared with the labour-power incorporated with them, is an expression of the growing productiveness of labour. The increase of the latter appears, therefore, in the diminution of the mass of labour in proportion to the mass of means of production moved by it, or in the diminution of the subjective factor of the labour process as compared with the objective factor.

This change in the technical composition of capital, this growth in the mass of means of production, as compared with the mass of the labour-power that vivifies them, is reflected again in its value-composition, by the increase of the constant constituent of capital at the expense of its variable constituent. There may be, e.g.originally 50 percent of a capital laid out in means of production, and 50 percent, in labour-power, later on, with the development of the productivity of labour, 80 percent, in means of production, 20 percent, in labour-power, and so on.

This law of the progressive increase in constant capital, in proportion to the variable, is confirmed at every step (as already shown) by the comparative analysis of the prices of commodities, whether we compare different economic epochs of different nations in the same epoch. The relative magnitude of the element of price, which represents the value of the means of production only, or the constant part of capital consumed, is in direct, the relative magnitude of the other element of price that pays labour (the variable part of capital) is in inverse proportion to the advance of accumulation.

This diminution in the variable part of capital as compared with the constant or the altered value-composition of the capital, however, only shows approximately the change in the composition of its material constituents.[2]

The above argument suggests that causes of unemployment is economic principle pursued by capitalists. If causes of unemployment and economic depression are dominated and controlled by the behavour of capitalists, entrepreneurs and people, Yamada Houkoku would argue the creation of Government enterprise based upon non-economic principle.

The reason is as follows. If non-economic principle dominates and controls the behavior of capitalists, entrepreneurs and people, this may lead to the increase in employment and output. Government enterprise based upon non-economic principle may stimulate the spirits of economic principle which exists within capitalists, entrepreneurs and people.

Unless capitalists believe that it is certain to get money from selling their products, they never increase employment and investment. The point is not the increase in effective demand or the increase in government expenditures but the increase in certainty, the decrease in uncertainty which exists within the mind of a capitalists and new investment which pays for a capitalist.

He would argue the creation of new industry which needs variable capital and creative innovation based upon current industry.

Unless consumers believe that they get salary on a constant basis, they reduce the amount of expenditures for consumption.

Notes
(1) See John Maynard Keynes, *The General theory of employment, Interest and money,* Macmillan, 1936, pp.23-34.
(2) See Karl Marx, *Capital : a critical analysis of capitalist production,* volume I, (chapter xxv, the general law of capitalist accumulation), Progress Publishers, 1887, pp.581-584.

Chapter 4
Macroeconomics and Relevance

4.1 Macroeconomics and relevance theory

Relevance theory developed by Deidre Wilson and Dan Sperber is related with the view that the characteristics of human communication is recognition and interpretation of intentions.[1] In human communication, a speaker provides evidence of her intention and the hearer tends to infer the speaker's intention on the basis of the evidence provided.

It automatically creates expectations which makes the hearer come closer to the speaker's intentions. The interpretation a rational hearer should choose must correspond to the meaning that best satisfies those expectations.

The central idea of relevance theory is that the expectations of relevance raised by an utterance make the hearer interpret the speaker's meaning precisely. According to relevance theory, an input such as a sight, a sound, an utterance and a memory is relevant to an individual. This means that if the input connects with background information, the hearer yields the conclusion which matters to him. In other words, an input or information becomes relevant to a hearer when his mental processing within a context of available assumptions produce a positive cognitive effect. Cognitive effect could be explained in the following example.

> On seeing my train arriving, I might look at my watch, access my knowledge of the train timetable, and derive the

contextual implication that my train is late which may itself achieve relevance by combining with further contextual assumptions to yield further implications. The sight of my train arriving late might confirm my impression that the service is deteriorating or make me alter my plans to do some shopping on the way to work.

The above example tells us that the sight of a train arriving one minute late make little difference and the sight of it arriving half an hour late makes much difference.[2] The relevance of information given vary according to cognitive effects and processing effort. In other words, as the positive cognitive effects achieved becomes greater, its relevance becomes greater. This means that as the effort of perception, memory and inference required becomes greater, cognitive attention or people's rewarding becomes less deserving. There is a trade-off relationship between processing effort and relevance of input.

One of the characteristics of relevance theory is that people tend to aim to maximize the relevance of the inputs one processes, because they like to make the most efficient use of the available processing resources. Relevance theory says that people tend to maximize relevance, because their cognitive systems have evolved and constant selection pressure increased efficiency. If we follow cognitive principle of relevance, human cognition tends to be directed toward the maximization of relevance. If this is true, economic policy-makers make it possible to predict and manipulate the mental states of private sector, provided they understand people's cognitive tendency to maximize relevance.

Relevance theory is a theory which goes beyond the probalistic model, because it proves that people's cognitive goal at a given moment is always maximizing the relevance of the information processed.

Relevance theory regards context not as given common ground but as a set of accessible items of information which are stored in short-term and encyclopedic memories or manifest in the physical environment. The assumption of relevance theory is that people select a context which maximizes relevance. In other words, in relevance theory, context is regarded as a variable.

Relevance theory proposes an account of the process of inferring relevant information from any given utterance.

An interpretation of a particular utterance depends upon the state of knowledge of a hearer and therefore it is relative or subjective. It involves working out the consequences of adding new information to old information, and therefore three cases would be considered.

(1) New information may weaken the assumption of old information.
(2) New information may strengthen the assumption of old information.
(3) New information may not affect the assumption of old information.

Relevance theory tells us that discretionary macroeconomic policy or government intervention policy such as fiscal policy, central bank's intervention in the forex market is not effective in some cases.

However, relevance theory also tells us that discretionary policy is effective in other cases. If macroeconomic policy is communication between government sector and private sector, discourse analysis, relevance theory, cognitive grammar, functional grammar, pragmatics in linguistics literature must be useful for the analysis of effect on macroeconomic policy.

In the utterance such as coffee would keep me awake, the speaker may want to stay awake amd drink coffee However, the host may assume that the speaker does not want to stay awake and drink coffee. Any economists may regard this misunderstanding as noise. However, pragmatists may disagree with this view and try to find out the mechanism of successful communication.

Yamada Houkoku would support discretionary macro-economic policy and policy-ineffectiveness of rational expectations hypothesis. The relation is as follows. Yamada Houkoku would also support relevance theory which tries to clarify expectations which make the hearer interpret the speaker's real intentions. It concludes that if each economic policy or each information announced by government is relevant, discretionary macroeconomic policy is effective, and on the other hand, if they are not relevant, Lucas' critique holds.

If we apply relevance theory to economic policy, the interpretation on government's announcement or macroeconomic policy a rational person should choose is the one that best meet his expectations. If they are relevant enough for private sector to be precise and predictable enough to be worthwhile making new investment, increasing employment and investing in financial assets, government's announcement or macroeconomic policy is effective. If a signal from government to private sector is relevant enough to change his behavior and then his processing in a context of available assumptions produces a positive cognitive effect.

They tells us that Deduction and inference in the context are important for the effectiveness of macroeconomic policy.

If deduction or inference occurs because of the union of new information and old information within human mind, then, the important thing for us to remember is that macroeconomic policy is effective if new information is not just the duplication of old information and, macroeconomic policy is not effective and people do not change their behavior if the added new information is just the duplication of old information. This means that macroeconomic policy takes contextual effect if the added new information is strongly connected with old information.

If contextual effect of macroeconomic policy is caused by the interaction between new information and old information, human cognition involves contextual implications, contradictions and strengthening. In other words, if we apply the concept of contextual implications, contradictions and strengthening to economic phenomenon. We could say that contextual contradiction such as financial depression or liquidity trap could be resolved by adding new information and contextual strengthening may mean financial bubble, overshooting of exchange rates and hyperinflation. Given Government's new macroeconomic policy, people selects the one conclusion that economy must start to get stronger and economy comes back to normal if there is a change in their cognitive environment. In other words, if government understands that people aim at cognitive efficiency, and make economic policy which drives them toward aiming at the most efficient information processing, then they make a self-organizing behavior and government do not need to increase fiscal deficit or change monetary policy.

Relevance theory analyses the situation when two assumptions are found to contradict each other. According to this theory, people tend to erase the weaker assumption if they compare their strengths. In other words, if people can't compare the strength of the two contradictory assumptions, then, the contradiction will be resolved by the addition of further evidence for or against one of the contradictory assumptions.

The concept of relevance could be explained by that of productivity, yield and cost-benefit analysis. If we assume that two firms achieve the same output with different inputs and different costs, then the firm with the lower production costs must be more productive.

Similar analysis can be applied to the analysis of relevance. People's cognitive abilities are limited and therefore, resources tend to be allocated to the processing of information which makes the greatest contribution to people's cognitive goals with the least processing effort.

Deirdre Wilson and Dan Sperber give us the following example.

> Mary and Peter are sitting on a park bench. He leans back, which alters her view. By leaning back, he modifies her cognitive environment, he reveals to her certain phenomena, which she may look at or not, and describe to herself in different ways. Why should she pay attention to one phenomenon rather than another or describe it to herself in one way rather than another? In other words, why should she mentally process any of the assumptions which have

become manifest or more manifest to her as a result of the change in her environment? Our answer is that she should process those assumptions that are most relevant to her at the time. Imagine, for instance, that as a result of Peter's leaning back she can see, among other things, three people: an ice-cream vendor who she had noticed before when she sat down on the bench, an ordinary stroller who she has never seen before, and her acquaintance William, who is coming toward them and is a dreadful bore.

Many assumptions about each of these characters are more or less manifest to her. She may already have considered the implications of the presence of the ice-cream vendor when she first noticed him, if so it would be a waste of processing resources to pay further attention to him now.

The presence of the unknown stroller is new information to her, but little or nothing follows from it, so there again, what she can perceive and infer about him is not likely to be of much relevance to her. By contrast, from the fact that William is coming her way, she can draw many conclusions from which many more conclusions will follow.

This, then is the one truly relevant change in her cognitive environment this is the particular phenomenon she should pay attention to, she should do so, that is, if she is aiming at cognitive efficiency.[3]

The above example tells us that unless people's behavior seem relevant enough to any person to be worth his attention, he does not pay attention to a phenomenon.

Mary assumes that Peter has good reason to think that she will get relevant information, by paying attention to Peter's behavior. Among the assumptions about the ice cream vendor, the stroller and William, Mary chooses the assumption of William, which she thinks, relevant enough to be worth her attention.

Notes
(1) See Dan Sperber and Deirdre Wilson
Relevance
communication and cognition (second edition)
Blackwell Publishing 1995
(2) See Dan Sperber and Deirdre Wilson.
See, Deirdre Wilson and Dan Sperber, "Relevance theory", G. Ward and L. Horn (eds.), *Handbook of Pragmatics,* Oxford Blackwell, 2008, pp.607-632.
(3) See Dan Sperber and Deirdre Wilson, pp.48-49.

4.2 Macroeconomics and some unpleasant rational expectations hypothesis

When we construct economic models it is important for economists to take into account the expectation of private agents about future policies. If the private sector forms expectations about future Government economic policy, the effect of economic policy would change and be different from that of economic policy makers' expectations. If the assumption of rational expectations hypothesis holds, the effect of macro-economic policy may be limited. The rational expectations hypothesis tells us that the interaction between the Government and the private sector, and the effect of expectations on economic policy is important and determines the effectiveness of macroeconomic policy. The interaction between the Government and the private sector depends upon Government future policy and the private sector's expectations about it. The effect of economic policy when the private sector has forward looking expectation, has been highlighted by the Lucas critique and the time-inconsistency problem. The assumption of rational expectations could be characterized by the relationship between rational expectation and dynamic game.

Maria Luisa Petit says in the following way.

> In both the Lucas critique and the time-inconsistency problem, behavioral decisions are the result of the optimization of given preference functions of economic agents.
>
> This optimization is performed by taking into account not only the current economic situation but also the expectations

about the economic situation in the future, expectations which are formed by using all available information. The use of econometric models for policy evaluation which describe the behavior of economic agents are not altered as a consequence of variations in the environment in which these agents operate.

And since a change in the policy rules constitutes a change in this environment, the above assumption implies that the behavioral relations of private agents are invariant under policy changes. Lucas maintains that this assumption is false for most existing macroeconometric models, methods of policy evaluation based upon macro econometric models can lead to serious errors since these models usually ignore the links between Government actions and private sector behavioral decisions.[1]

The Lucas critique criticizes the Keynesian macro econometric models and discretionary macroeconomic policy. However, although the argument that a change in the policy rules, a change in economic environment alters the behaviour of economic agents, Keynesian macro econometric models whose assumption is that the behavior of economic agents are constant, even in the case of a change of policy rule, may be right.

Keynesian discretionary economic policy may be effective although people's expectation are rational if economic policy alters the behavior of economic agents and it follows the behavior which government wants.

It might be unfair to criticize Keynes's economic theory in terms of expectations, because the general theory emphasizes the importance of expectations about future profits, which is strongly related to business cycle, economic boom and slump.[2]

Economic boom occurs, provided that profit expectations are high and interest rate expectations are low.

If government economic policy leads to high profit expectations and low interest rate, discretionary economic policy must be effective. The point for us to discuss here is not whether discretionary economic policy is effective or not. The important thing for us to discuss is economic assumption itself, and how people make decisions and make a forecast in an uncertain environment.

J.M. Keynes's assumption is not based upon adaptive expectations or rational expectations. Its assumption is based upon relevance theory. Thomas J. Sargent says in the following way.

> If there is a change in monetary regime, that is, a switch in the money supply rule, the economic model predicts that the Granger-causality structure of the money-inflation process will change.
>
> In this sense, since changes in the stochastic process for money creation are supposed to produce predictable changes in the stochastic process for inflation, money "causes" inflation. This means that money creation is not exogenous with respect to inflation.[3]

In other words, money creation is endogenous with respect to inflation. On the other hand, we should try to clarify economic conditions that economic variables become endogenous and change people's expectations and their behaviors. We also should tries to create the economic concept of some unpleasant rational expectation's hypothesis, named after Thomas J. Sargent's "some unpleasant monetarist arithmetic". He corrects the monetarist model to include a more sophisticated and dynamic description of the demand for base money and concludes that tighter money may lead to a higher inflation.

Thomas J. Sargent says in the following way.

After World War I, Germany owed staggering reparations to the allied countries. This fact dominated Germany's public finance from 1919 until 1923 and was a most important force for hyperinflation.

The event of stabilization was attended by a monetary reform in which on 15 October 1923 a new currency unit called the Renten mark was declared equivalent to 1 trillion paper marks.

While great psychological significance has sometimes been assigned to this unit change, it is difficult to attribute any substantial effects to what was in itself only a cosmetic measure. The substantive aspect of the decree of October 15 was the establishing of a Renten bank to take over the note issue functions of the Renten bank. The decree put binding limits upon both the total volume of rentenmarks that could be issued, 3.2 billion marks, and the maximum amount that could be issued to the government, 1.2 billion marks. This limitation on the amount of credit that could be extended to the government was announced at a time when the government was financing virtually 100 percent of its expenditures by means of note issue.

In December 1923, the management of the Renten bank was tested by the government and effectively made clear its intent to meet its obligation to limit government borrowing to within the amount decreed simultaneously and abruptly three things happened: additional government borrowing from the central bank stopped, the government budget swung into balance and inflation stopped.

The dramatic progress toward a balanced budget that was made in the months after the Renten bank decree. The government moved to balance the budget by taking a series of deliberate, permanent actions to raise taxes and eliminate expenditures. Substantially aiding the fiscal situation, Germany also obtained relief from her reparation obligations. Reparations payments were temporarily suspended, and the Dawes plan assigned Germany a much more manageable schedule of payments.

The substantial growth of central bank note and demand deposit liabilities in the months after the currency was stabilized. the best explanation for this is that at the margin the post inflation increase in notes was no longer backed by government debt. Instead, in the German case, it was largely backed by discounted commercial bills. The nature of the system of promises and claims behind the central bank's liabilities changed when after the Renten bank decree the central bank no longer offered additional credit to the government.

So once again the interpretation of the time series on central bank notes and deposits must undergo a very substantial change. By all available measures the stabilization of the German mark was accompanied by increase in output and employment and decreases in unemployment.[4]

What he emphasizes is that economic policies that ended hyperinflation in Germany were interrelated and coordinated, and the creation of an independent central bank refused the government's demand for additional unsecured credit.

The above argument and analysis suggests the importance of people's cognition, assumption, and interpretation of given context and information.

The theory of rational expectations does not tell us how to make people's expectation rational. The hypothesis of rational expectations is based upon the assumption that people understand economic laws. However, if people do not understand economic laws, this means that they can not make a rational decision when they are faced with the rule of change. The point is not how people behave and make decisions in a dynamic set within a economic constraint, but how they assume that the future of economy changes as the rule of change or policy regimes change. That strongly depends upon people's knowledge or people's cognition.

Yamada Houkoku's concern is related with the following points.

(1) changing people's knowledge or perception.

(2) each economic policy must be relevant.

(3) making people's expectation rational.

Economic policy of Yamada Houkoku can be characterized by the following argument.

(1) Keynesian discretionary macroeconomic policy is effective if monetary policy and fiscal policy are relevant.

(2) The creation of government enterprise creates effective demand which contributes to the reduced unemployment and stimulates private enterprise to increase investment

and employment.

(3) Government stops intervening in the market when economy comes back to normal.

Notes

(1) See Maria Luisa Petit, *Control theory and dynamic games in economic policy analysis*, Cambridge University Press, 2009.

(2) See Walter Allan, *A critique of Keynesian Economics,* St. Martin's Press, 1992.

(3) See Thomas J. Sargent, *Rational expectations and inflation,* Harper Collins College Division, 1986.

(4) See Thomas J. Sargent, *Rational expectations and inflation,* Harper Collins College Division, 1986, pp.79-93.

4.3 Macroeconomics and liquidity trap

George Soros recognizes that our understanding of the world is inherently imperfect and emphasizes the importance of fallibility.

Soros assumes that our understanding of reality is based upon our imperfect knowledge. When we consider the relationship between thinking and reality, our imperfect knowledge makes our understanding imperfect. Soros says that our interpretation based upon our imperfect knowledge affect the events which affect our understanding and knowledge, natural science and social science are different in the sense that natural science is not affected by what we think, and social science is affected by what we think. Soros emphasizes that thinking and reality is reflexive and thinking creates reality which creates new thinking and therefore, thinking and reality are indispensable. According to Soros, reflexivity is relevant and it introduces an element of uncertainty, both into the participants' understanding and into the events in which they participate. In other words, the participants' imperfect understanding based upon their imperfect knowledge introduces an uncertain element into the situation in which they participate.

Events occurs because, people thinks, unlike natural science, social events are based upon thinking participants. Different people have different opinions about the situations even if they face the same situation, and therefore the relationship between thinking and reality is very complicated. Soros says that there is a two-way interaction between the thinking participants and the events or situation.

Soros explains the theory of reflexivity in the following way.

The divergence between the events and expectations tends to affect the participants' bias. In financial markets, a positive feedback reinforce the participants' bias, which contribute to a prevailing bias. However, if the gap between the events and expectations or the participant's bias continues, the reflexive process doesn't last forever. If the participant changes his self-perception and this will affect the outcome soon.

Changes in current expectations could affect the future movement of financial assets such as currency, stocks and bonds.

Soros says that financial world is not rational, unstable and chaotic. This means that mathematical formula does not determine changes of prices in the financial market. What we think about the situations is part of what we think about, and if this is true, our thinking lacks objectivity. According to Soros, our views of the world are always flawed and distorted. The rational school and the efficient market hypothesis argues that traders have perfect knowledge of a company, therefore every share is valued at the correct price and all stock prices reflect available information.

Soros has some doubts about the thought of classical economics, the concept of equilibrium, perfect competition, and perfect knowledge. He strongly argues that the decision to make investment is based upon expectations and an imperfect understanding of the world.[1]

If an imperfect understanding creates the events, the economy is always in disequilibrium. If we follow the view of Soros, the bias of traders toward currency or stock creates the price movements. The resulting price movement leads to the underlying trends to affect traders' expectations. The hypothesis of rational expectations explains how people form expectations about economic variables and argues the ineffectiveness of discretionary macroeconomic policy.

On the other hand, relevance theory explains how people form expectations in an optimal way, given their limited cognitive resources and the uncertainties of economic environment and argues the effectiveness and ineffectiveness of discretionary macroeconomic policy.

Paul Krugman says in the following way.

> If the economy will, in fact, be in the liquidity trap, and in that case, any further increase in the money supply will have no effect. Monetary expansion is irrelevant, because the private sector does not expect it to be sustained, because they believe that given a chance, the central bank will revert to type and stabilize prices. What is needed is a central bank commitment to steady positive monetary growth, which will encourage inflationary expectations and lower expected real interest rates.[2]

On the other hand, Yamada Houkoku would analyse the liquidity trap in terms of relevance or irrelevance. In other words, monetary expansion is irrelevant because the private sector does not increase investment, employment and spending, because he assumes that monetary expansion is not relevant with economic recovery, increased purchasing power, permanent life employment and rising prices etc.

His view is that only a central bank commitment to steady positive monetary growth does not encourage inflationary expectations and change people's expectations.

Economic policy of Yamada Houkoku is based upon the assumption that the selection of a particular context such as economic recovery from financial depression is determined by people's search for relevance. And therefore if people does not assume that a central bank commitment to steady positive monetary growth is relevant to economic recovery, their increased salary, the increased amount of economic goods purchased, only the commitment may not be effective with respect to output and employment.

The General Theory developed by J. M. Keynes emphasizes the importance of expectations in economic fluctuations. However, he ignores the importance of cognition in economic fluctuations. On the other hand, economic policy of Yamada Houkoku assumes that people's expectations depend upon people's cognition and their interpretation of context in economic environment. And therefore, the purpose of his economic policy is to change people's interpretations of context in economic environment.

He would not criticize the classical theory, neoclassical economics, new classical economics. Houkokunomics proposes the creation of government enterprise on an international level in order to make the assumptions of the classical theory of economics hold.

J. M. Keynes says in the following way.

> the postulates of the classical theory are applicable to a special case only and not to the general case, the situation which it assumes being a limiting point of the possible positions of equilibrium.
>
> Our criticism of the accepted classical theory of economics

has consisted not so much in finding logical flaws in its analysis as in pointing out that its tacit assumptions are seldom or never satisfied, with the result that it cannot solve the economic problems of the actual world.[3]

However, if we make its tacit assumptions satisfied, this means that Government does not need to intervene in the market. The point is how we should make its tacit assumptions satisfied.

J. M. Keynes's analyses the marginal efficiency of capital in terms of the expectation of yield, the current supply price of the capital asset and the rate of return expected.

If the actual results of the production and sale of output is relevant to employment in so far as they cause a modification of subsequent expectations and then people modify their expectations if government enterprise increase the purchase of goods from a private sector.

If the expectations of changes in the value of money influences the volume of current output, stimulates investment, and increases the schedule of the marginal efficiency of capital then, their prospective yield and changes in the expectation of their prospective yield increases.

J. M. Keynes says in the following way.

> Even apart from the instability due to speculation, there is the instability due to the characteristic of human nature that a large proportion of our positive activities depend on spontaneous optimism rather than on a mathematical expectation, and animal spirits of a spontaneous urge to action rather than inaction. The marginal efficiency of capital depends upon current expectations as to the future

yield of capital-goods. Economic booms are characterized by optimistic expectations as to the future yield of capital goods.

When disillusion falls upon an overoptimistic and overbought market. the dismay and uncertainty as to the future which accompanies a collapse in the marginal efficiency of capital naturally precipitates a sharp increase in liquidity-preference and hence a rise in the rate of interest. Thus the fact that a collapse in the marginal efficiency of capital tends to be associated with a rise in the rate of interest may seriously aggravate the decline in investment. The collapse in the marginal efficiency of capital is so strong that a reduction in the rate of interest is not capable of providing an effective remedy for economic recovery. To revive the marginal efficiency of capital is not easy, because of the uncontrollable and disobedient psychology of the business world.[4]

When the return of confidence, which is related with the reliability of the prospective yield, is needed, economic policy of Yamada Houkoku unlike the economics of Keynes, proposes the following economic solutions.
(1) government enterprise increases the purchasing price of goods from a private sector.
(2) government creates government enterprises which lend money, promise to purchase goods, export them, and increase the market for exchange in order for the confidence and the prospective yield to increase.

The economics of Keynes depends upon the following points.
(1) the principle of effective demand

(2) expectation and employment
(3) the marginal propensity to consume and the multiplier
(4) the marginal efficiency of capital
(5) the state of long-term expectation
(6) incentives to liquidity

Economic policy of Yamada Hokoku depends upon the following points.
(1) the market of exchange
(2) the number of economic network
(3) fractal-based economic system
(4) comparative advantage
(5) purchasing power of money
(6) "certain" economic system in the sense that government enterprises purchase goods from a private sector
(7) an invisible demand

According to economic policy of Yamada Houkoku, the necessity of central controls to bring about an adjustment between the propensity to consume and the inducement to invest is met by the creation of government enterprises which purchase economic goods from private enterprise and increase employment.

According to his economic policy, one of the causes of economic depression is not lack of effective demand but lack of the market of exchange for economic goods or services due to financial collapse or reduced purchasing power of money. Therefore, even if government spends huge amount of money, the effect is limited or even little.

The creation of international "Buikukyoku" is expected to prevent each country from engaging in international competition, and correct mismatch between demand and supply. If we define Adam Smith's invisible hand as the smooth functioning of the market for exchange and match between supply and demand in time and place, economic recovery from financial depression must be related with not only fiscal and monetary policy but also the creation of government enterprise which creates the smooth functioning of the market for exchange, match between supply and demand, increase the number of division of labour, exchange the old currency with the new currency whose value is higher than the old one, increases the number of economic networks or connections, creates the new creative innovated goods and increases economic diversity which creates economic diversity.

Yamada Houkoku would say that the creation of mutual interaction through the exchange of other goods is expected to create economic diversity and creative innovation.

He is influenced by not only Western economics but also Eastern world view and traditions.

If one of the most important characteristics of his economic policy is that it emphasizes the importance of interconnection and interdependence.

Notes
(1) See George Soros, *Open society : Reforming Global Capitalism,* Little, Brown and Company, 2000.
(2) Paul Krugman, "Thinking about the liquidity trap",
http://www.mit. cdu/Krugman/www/trioshrt.htm/1999
(3) See John Maynard Keynes, *The General Theory of Employment, interest and money,* Macmillan, 1936, p.3, p.378.
(4) See John Maynard Keynes, pp.161-164, pp.313-332.

Postscript
Great Depression, Financial Crisis and Houkokunomics, baced upon Economic Mind of Yamada Houkoku

In my view, the creation of international stabilization fund is necessary for the growth and stability of world economy. Speculators such as investment banks start to buy financial assets such as stocks or currency when their prices start to rise and therefore their speculations lead to an escalating rise in prices.

It may cause the crash of stock market or currency market. International stabilization fund does not intervene in the market, provided that the price of stock or currency starts to fall rapidly.

The analysis of financial market based upon a microeconomic foundation suggests that the collapse of bubble can be explained by the imbalance between the number of sellers and the number of buyers. Therefore, the purpose of international stabilization fund is to correct this imbalance. In other words, international stabilization fund works out stabilizing speculation and speculators work out destabilizing speculation.

What I would like to emphasize strongly is that international stabilization fund promises to buy currency or stocks from speculators at the same price which they bought. This means that they never lose money. International stabilization fund also promises to buy economic goods from private sectors and lend money to them when economic depression or deflation means that people hardly buy economic goods and save more money.

If international stabilization fund promises to buy economic goods, lend money to manufactures for investments and recommends them to make more investment and employ more people, economic slump may change into economic boom soon.

The question now arises why international stabilization fund has enough money to buy economic goods, currency or stock and lend money.

The reason can be explained as follows. International stabilization fund is not simply a financial institution, because it tries to make huge profits in order to take advantage of price differentials between the selling price and buying price of economic goods, currency and stocks. This means that it tries to export economic goods it bought at the higher price to countries or domestic regions.

Keynes's largest influence came from a book called The general theory of employment interest and money.

Keynes's basic idea can be explained as follows. Governments have to run deficits when the economy is in economic depression, because the private sector will not invest enough to keep people fully employed. People tend to reduce their investments as their markets become satisfied and therefore a vicious cycle such as less investment, few jobs, less consumption and deflation occurs.

If people suffer from a failure of consumer demand which arises out of a lack of purchasing power, governments have to make additions to the purchasing power of people, by creating effective demand, in Keynes's view. Therefore, Keynes opposed balancing the fiscal budget, although many economists of the time supported balanced budgets. On the other hand, Keynes criticized the view that government deficits are not necessary to avoid high unemployment.

Houkoku's economic idea and Keynes's economic idea seem to be quite similar in the sense that government have to intervene in the market and put lots of money into the economy to keep people fully employed. However, there is a great difference between them in the sense that in Keynes's idea, fiscal deficit is obliged to increase and in Houkoku's idea, fiscal surplus is obliged to increase.

Afterword

George Lakoff and Mark Johnson say in the following way.

Classical mathematics comprises an objectivist universe. It has entities that are clearly distinguished from one another, e.g. numbers. Mathematical entities have inherent properties, e.g. three is odd. And there are fixed relationships among those entities, e.g. nine is the square of three. Mathematical logic was developed as part of the enterprise of providing foundations for classical mathematics.

Formal semantics also developed out of that enterprise. The models used in formal semantics are examples of what we will call "objectivist models" models appropriate to universes of discourse where there are distinct entities which have inherent properties and where there are fixed relationships among the entities.

But the real world is not an objectivist universe, especially those aspects of the real world having to do with human beings : human experience, human institutions, human language, the human conceptual system. What it means to be a hard-core objectivist is to claim that there is an objectivist model that fits the world as it really is.

We have just argued that objectivist philosophy is empirically incorrect in that it makes false predictions about language, truth, understanding, and the human conceptual system. On the basis of this we have claimed that objectivist philosophy provides an inadequate basis for the human sciences.

Nonetheless, a lot of remarkably insightful logicians,

linguists, psychologists, and computer scientists have designed objectivist models for use in the human sciences. We are claiming no such thing we believe that objectivist models as mathematical entities do not necessarily have to be tied to objectivist philosophy One can believe that objectivist models can have a function even an important function in the human sciences without adopting the objectivist premise that there is an objectivist model that completely and accurately fits the world as it really is. But if we reject this premise, what role is left for objectivist models? (George Lakoff and Mark Johnson, *Metaphors We Live By,* The university of Chicago Press, 1980, pp.218-219.)

His economic idea could be explained by the above argument.

Human thought processes are metaphorical and structured by human concepts. If this is true, the effectiveness of macroeconomic policy depends upon human concepts, which control thought, perception and action. If we regard economic policy as communication between government or people and economic recovery or economic depression as people's response against changed economic variables, common knowledge or assumption shared between government and people really counts in communication and response.

He shall argue that the ineffectiveness of economic policy does represent misunderstanding between government and people in common knowledge, assumptions and values. A coin has two sides: a bright side and a negative side. In a similar way, human cognitive abilities allow people to focus upon only one aspect of the economic situation. Focusing upon only one aspect means ignoring other aspects.

If policy ineffectiveness or economic depression is due to people's focusing upon only one aspect, he would emphasize the importance of making people focus upon other aspects.

References

Adam Smith, *The Wealth of Nations,* A Bantam Book, 2003.
Andrew Walter, *World power and world money,* Harvester Wheatsheaf, 1993.
Ben S. Bernanke, *Essays on the Great Depression,* Princeton University Press, 2000.
Costantino Bresciani-turroni, *The economics of inflation : a study of currency depreciation in post-war Germany,* George Allen & Unwin, 1937.
Dan Sperber and Deidre Wilson, *Relevance : Communication and cognition,* Blackwell Publishing, 1995.
David Lee, *Cognitive Linguistics introduction,* Oxford University Press, 2001.
Deirde Wilson and Dan Sperber, "Relevance Theory", G. Ward and L.Horn(eds.), *Handbook of Pragmatics,* Oxford Blackwell 2008, pp.607-632.
Edwin O. Reischauer, *Japan : The story of a nation,* Charles E Tuttle Co. Publishers, 1990.
Fritjof Capra, *The Tao of physics : an exploration of the parallels between modern physics and Eastern,* Mysticism, 1999.
George Soros, *Open society : Reforming Global Capitalism,* Little, Brown and Company, 2000.
G.C Allen, *Modern Japan and its problems,* The Athlone Press, 1990.
Goodhart, C. A.E., *Money, Information and uncertainty,* Macmillan, 1989.
Jean-Pierre Lehmann, *The roots of modern Japan,* The Macmillan Press, 1982.
Geoffrey N. Leech, *Principles of Pragmatics,* Longman, 1983.
John Maynard Keynes, *A tract on monetary reform,* Pronetheus books, 2000.
John Maynard Keynes, *The General theory of employment : Interest and money,* Macmillan, 1936.
John Kenneth Galbraith, *The Great Crash 1929,* Houghtom Mibblim company, 1997.
John Whitney Hall, *The Cambridge History of Japan,* volume 4, Early Modern Japan, Cambridge University Press, 1991.
Karl Marx, *Capital : a critical analysis of capitalist production,* volume 1, Progress Publishers, 1887.
Krugman, Paul, "Thinking about the liquidity trap",
    http://www.mit.edu/krugman/www/trioshrt.htm/
K. Alec Chrystal and Paul D. Mizen, "Goodhart Law: Its origins, Meaning and implications for monetary policy"

http://cyberlibris.typepad.com/blog/files/Goodharts-Law.pdf
Irving Fisher, *The monetary illusion,* Adelphi Company, 1927.
Lien-Sheng Yang, *Money and credit in China,* Harvard University Press, 1952.
Lakoff, George and Mark Johnson, *Metaphors we live by,* University of Chicago Press, 1980.
Lakoff,George, *Women, Fire and Dangerous things : What categories reveal about the mind,* University of Chicago Press, 1987.
Phra Sarasas, *Money and Banking in Japan,* Health Cranton Limited, 1940.
Peter Frost, *The Bakumatsu currency crisis,* Harvard University Press, 1970.
Peter Grundy, *Doing Pragmatics,* Arnold, 1995.
Peter Grundy, *Doing Pragmatics,* Oxford University Press, 2000.
Marius B. Jansen, *The Cambridge History of Japan, volume* ~, The nineteenth century, Cambridge university Press, 1989.
Maria Luisa Petit, *Control theory and dynamic games in economic policy analysis,* Cambridge University Press, 1990.
Ronald W. Langacker, *Concept, Image and Symbol the cognitive basis of grammar,* Mouton De Gruyter, 1990.
Robert E Lucas and Thomas J. Sargent (eds.), *Rational expectations : Econometric practice,* University of Minnesota Press, 1981.
Ronald W. Langacker, *Foundations of cognitive grammar,* volume 1, theoretical prerequisites, Stanford University Press, 1987.
Robert Slater, *Soros The Life, Times and Trading : Secrets of the World's Greatest Investor,* McGraw-Hill, 1996.
Thomas C. Smith, *The Agrarian Origins of Modern Japan,* Stanford, 1959.
Thomas J. Sargent, *Rational expectations and inflation,* Harper Collins College Division, 1986.
Patrick Minford, "expectations and the economy", Walter Allan (ed.), *A critique of Keynesian Economics,* St. Martin's press, 1992.
Vivian Cook and Mark Newson, *Chomsky's Universal Grammar,* Blackwell, 1996.
Ulric Neisser, *Cognition and Reality principles and implications of cognitive psychology,* W.H, Freeman and company, 1976.

Part II

On the Economics of J. M. Keynes, New Classical Economics and Generative Economics:
"A study in Relevance, Cognition and Macroeconomic Theory"

Preface

J. M. Keynes emphasizes the paradox of poverty in General Theory. The paradox of poverty means that as the community becomes richer, the gap between its actual and its potential production becomes larger.

In other words, a very modest measure of investment will be sufficient to provide full employment in a poor community.

On the other hand, the inducement to invest is weak and therefore the working of the principle of effective demand tends to reduce actual output in a wealthy community.

Although General Theory by J. M. Keynes is a great achievement, he does not provide an adequate answer for economic problems which I mentioned above.

The new classical economics and the rational expectations school challenged the Keynesian view of the world. However this does not mean that J. M. Keynes's view of the world is wrong.

The point is to clarify how J. M. Keynes might have developed and modified General Theory if he were alive now.

J. M. Keynes emphasizes uncertainty and expectation and therefore new classical economics and rational expectations school have not challenged J. M. Keynes's view of the world.

Globalization makes the capitalists behave on a strong economic principle and economic efficiency. A strong economic principle implies the increase in the number of part-time workers and low wage workers.

If J. M. Keynes were alive now, he would propose the creation of government enterprise which is not based upon economic efficiency or economic principle and might say that a fractal-based economic system must be the answer for our prosperity in a global age.

The reason is as follows.

There is a proportionate relationship between an increase in real income and an increase in consumption.

Unlike Milton Friedman, inflation or deflation may be just a phenomenon of degee of relevance. This means that a capitalist may change a selling price of his products in order to maximize their profits and his decision may depend upon his view of the world.

In other words, if he decreases a selling price and his profits do not increase, then he may try to decrease it further. On the other hand, if he increases a selling price and his profits do not decrease, then he may try to increase a selling price further.

If inflation or deflation is purely a cognitive phenomenon, Government enterprise should purchase economic goods when their prices are low and sells them when their prices are high in order to stabilize the price level and change people's cognition.

J. M. Keynes says in the following way.

> To choose a higher value for the franc might disturb the equilibrium of the Budget which has been so painfully achieved. It would upset the industrialist exporters-who have their means of exerting political influence. And most tangible of all it would involve the Bank of France in a loss on the foreign exchange said to amount to some £ 300,000,000, which, as an agent of the Government, it has bought up at the present rate.
>
> To fix 100 francs to the, for example, might cost the Bank

of France £60,000,000 of which no mean proportion might accrue to foreigners. This is just the sort of argument which M Poincare and every other Frenchman is able to understand. The deed, therefore is done. Since it removes an element of uncertainty from the money markets and stock exchanges of the world and since French importers and manufactures need hesitate no longer, a good deal of purchasing power, which has been lying idle, may be returned to active employment. M Poincare has therefore done something-perhaps for the first time in his career-to make the rest of us feel more cheerful.[1]

The arguments mentioned above say that J. M. Keynes emphasizes the importance of removing an element of uncertainty.

I believe that the creation of Government enterprise and a fractal-based economic system leads to the removal of an element of uncertainty.

Yasuhisa Miyake
August, 2012

Note
(1) See John Maynard Keynes, *Essays in Persuasion,* Macmillan, 1931, pp.115-116.

Foreword

The purpose of this book is to discuss our argument that only monetary and fiscal policy is not enough for us to achieve economic recovery.

This book might have proved that only monetary and fiscal policy is not enough for us to achieve economic recovery. On the other hand, if we define economic depression as economic phenomenon that a reduction in the amount of goods exchanged is due to the fact that people assume that their purchasing power in money is decreasing, then, economic solution for economic prosperity must be to increase their purchasing power in money.

If we define economic boom as economic phenomenon that an increase in the amount of goods exchanged is due to the fact that people assume that their purchasing power in money is increasing. Deflation means that their real purchasing power in money increases. However money illusion might contribute to economic depression, that a reduction in nominal income makes them believe that their purchasing power in money decreases.

Faced with economic depression and deflation they might pay more attention to a reduction in nominal income rather than their purchasing power in money.

On the other hand, faced with economic boom and inflation, they might pay more attention to an increase in commodity prices, stocks and nominal income rather than their real purchasing power in money.

If they assume that a further decrease in their purchasing power in money continues in the future, only monetary and fiscal policy are not effective with respect to output and employment.

If we apply cognitive linguistics and relevance theory to the explanation of economic fluctuations, our view of the economy, our attention, our way of interpreting new information change over time, depending upon our emotional state in a specific context.

In other words, if we are in an optimistic mood, our attention tends to be concerned with a further increase in stock prices and commodity prices. If we are in a pessimistic mood, our attention tends to be concerned with a further reduction in nominal income.

For example, new information has two sides. However, we tend to pay attention to only one aspect of information depending upon a specific context or a given situation. This means that we might ignore a change in policy regimes such as a fiscal expenditure, a higher interest rate, a lower interest rate, an increase in money supply and a decrease in money supply, depending upon a given situation. If this is true, the important thing for economic policy makers to do is to make them pay more attention to real purchasing power in money or to make them assume that their purchasing power is increasing definitely and that a capitalist's profit and demand are increasing definitely. What I want to emphasize is that a concrete proposal for achieving such a goal is to create a public enterprise whose purpose is to make a price adjustment mechanism work smoothly, to exchange old currency with new currency in order to increase their purchasing power in money and to increase effectual demand, not effective demand.

Current macroeconomics emphasizes the importance of expectation.

Economics of J. M. Keynes and new classical economics are quite the same in the sense that both of them involve the importance of expectation. However, they ignore the importance of cognition and schema, although a signal effect, announcement effects and a dynamic inconsistency may involve cognition and schema.[1]

Therefore it may be very important for us to discuss and analyze economic policy in terms of relevance theory and cognitive linguistics.

Economic policy involves a kind of interaction. This means that economic policy affects each economic player differently. The reason is that different players have different knowledge, different values and different interpretations.

In other words, the effect of economic policy involves uncertainty and it can't control them exclusively.

This uncertainty involves the values, interpretations, knowledge, schema of each individual economic player, and the interaction between economic policy and them.

In other words, economic policy at the previous period affects the effect of current economic policy, It affects the values, interpretation, knowledge and schema of each individual in the future. The creation of public enterprise which reduces uncertainty and increase certainty encourages a firm to increase investment, output and employment. It does not matter whether an ideal government should be a big one or a cheap one.

The important thing is that a government produces profits or wealth, which results in the fact that this contributes to an increase in the profits of a private firm.

If we apply the economic policy of Yamada Houkoku to the solutions of current economic problems, the following explanations can be written down.

The central banks borrow money form commercial banks and they lend money to a public firm which purchases economic goods from a private firm. Yamada Houkoku solves the economic problem of a disequilibrium between saving, investment and consumption. In a capitalist economy, consumers make a decision about their savings independently and capitalists make a decision about their investments independently.

As John Maynard Keynes says, one of the causes of economic depression might be a disequilibrium between saving, investment and consumption.[2]

The objective of consumers is different from that of capitalists. Consumers try to maximize their utility, in order to follow their economic principle. Capitalists try to maximize their utility in order to follow their economic principle.

Faced with economic depression, consumers try to save more and this leads to the fact that capitalists can't maximize their utility, In other words, this makes economic depression worse and it changes into great depression, The creation of economic web whose objective of public enterprise, private firm, and consumer is in the same direction and they are interdependent each other, is necessary to solve a disequilibrium between saving, investment and consumption. Faced with economic depression, a market mechanism or a small government might not be the answer for economic recovery.

In a market economy, its smooth functioning depends upon the degree of risk, uncertainty, and the degree of difference of economic objectives between consumers, producers, and capitalists, Therefore, to reduce the degree of them might be the answer for economic recovery. Economic policy of Yamada Houkoku gives us the following economic solutions.

(1) How to increase the amount of goods exchanged and prevent price competition between firms and a low price selling from occurring.

(2) How to make a domestic country's export to a foreign country contribute to the increase in employment in the country.

(3) How to reduce the amount of firms which decrease the amount of money for employers in order to maximize their profits within a critical number.

(4) How to make effective demand and effectual demand increase, not depending upon a huge government deficit, and a fiscal expenditure.

(5) How to make the least government intervention in order to reduce the amount of employment.

(6) How to increase multiplier effect.

(7) How to reduce a disequilibrium between investment and saving.

(8) How to create "creative innovation" which means that new innovation creates demand for commodity A which leads to commodity B.

Note

(1) J. M. Keynes seems to have recognized the importance of cognition and schema.

> "In general, however, a change in circumstances or expectations will cause some realignment in individual holdings of money since, in fact, a change will influence different individuals differently by reason partly of differences in environment and the reason for which money is held and partly

of differences in environment and the reason for which money is held and partly of differences in knowledge and interpretation of the new situation". (John Maynard Keynes, *The general theory of employment, interest and money,* Prometheus Books, 1997, p.198)

(2) Axel Leijonhufuud says in the following way.

"Keynes, in contrast to the classics, emphasized that saving decisions and investment decisions are typically made by different people. Although the classics were aware of the fact, they did not perceive its significance, Keynes realized that it had an extremely important implication. namely that it is not at all certain that planned saving and planned investment will be equal at a full employment level of income. Thus, in this neglected fact lay the key to the Keynesian Revolution, to be rightly understood, this exegetical argument should be supplied with a number of provisos. Thus, one might consider a hypothetical economy entirely devoid of intra-private-sector credit markets so that saving and investment must be undertaken by the same people, and then ask whether Keynes's analysis of the income-constrained process would be entirely irrelevant to such a system. The answer is that such a process is quite possible, since a situation of aggregate ante hoarding may still emerge with planned saving exceeding investment. As for the "classics", the problem which was their constant concern was defined exactly in the above manner-.i.e.in a market system, decisions to produce and decisions to consume (or to hold) any good whatsoever are made by "different people "and will not be consistent purely by chance.

Thus the peculiarity of the saving-investment process does not lie in the fact that the decisions are made by different groups of people.

That Keynesian processes are extremely unlikely to occur in a crusoe-economy is after all a trivial point. In order to justify the emphasis which Keynes put on the saving-investment process, one must take into account the arguments he adduced in support of the contention that existing market institutions are especially inadequate when it comes to the task of coordinating these decisions. If saving and investment decisions were in fact always undertaken by the same people, a closed system would be quite unlikely to fall into serious recession, because of a decline of the marginal efficiency of capital (or a decline in the propensity to consume)". (Axel Leijonhufuud, *On Keynesian Economics and the economics of Keynes : a study in monetary theory,* Oxford University press, 1968, pp.362-363)

Yamada Houkoku created the economic situations whose saving and investment decisions were in fact always undertaken by the same people.

Chapter 1
A Critical View of General Theory

J. M. Keynes says in the following way.

> From the time of Say and Ricardo the classical economists have taught that supply creates its own demand-meaning by this in some significant, but not clearly defined, sense that the whole of the costs of production must necessarily be spent in the aggregate, directly or in directly, on purchasing the product.
>
> In J. S. Mill's principle of Political Economy the doctrine is expressly set forth.
>
> What constitutes the means of payment for commodities are simply commodities.
>
> Each person's means of paying for the productions of other people consist of those which he himself possesses. All sellers are inevitably, and by the meaning of the world, buyers.
>
> Could we suddenly double the productive powers of the country, we should double the supply of commodities in every market, but we should, by the same stroke, double the purchasing power. Everybody would bring a double demand as well as supply, everybody would be able to buy twice as much, because one would twice as much to offer in exchange.[1]

What J. M. Keynes emphasizes in the arguments mentioned above is that those which people possesses does not hold as a means of paying for the productions of other people in a capitalist economy because it is a monetary economy.

In other words, if a capitalist economy is not a monetary economy, then the argument mentioned above holds.

The analysis mentioned above implies that a monetary economy itself is inherently unstable in the sense that it may hinder an exchange of goods and contribute to the reduced output and employment, However, the General Theory by J. M. Keynes does not provide any solutions for a unstable monetary system. J. M. Keynes emphasizes the importance of monetary and fiscal policy. However, the important thing for us is to create a stable economic system, which involves the well-functioning of an exchange of goods and contributes to the increase in output and employment.

J. M. Keynes tends to analyse a capitalist economy in terms of a marginal propensity to consume investment and aggregate demand. He emphasizes the fundamental psychological law and says that men are disposed to increase their consumption as their income increases, but not by as much as the increase in their income.

If there is a proportional relationship between the increase in real income and the increase in consumption, this may contribute to the increase in output and employment.

One of the real causes of unemployment is the fact that the marginal propensity to consume tends to decrease as economy reaches to full employment. This means that it is difficult for us to secure a further increase of employment by increasing investment.

Economic solution for unemployment might be to change the paradoxical conclusion that a poor community is more subject to violent fluctuations than a wealthy community, because saving is a larger proportion of income and the multiplier is smaller in a wealthy community.

In J. M. Keynes's view, a further increase in investment does not contribute to the increase of employment because the marginal propensity to consume is low in a wealthy community.

On the other hand, if the number and amount of division of labor or exchange of goods is the function of employment, then a further increase in investment may not lead to the increase of employment even if the marginal propensity to consume is high, Central controls to bring about an adjustment between the propensity to consume and the inducement to invest may not contribute to the increase of employment and output. J. M. Keynes's emphasizes the importance of knowledge and interpretation of the new situation. However, a traditional Keynesian models ignores it, The new classical economics and the rational exportations school have emphasized the importance of expectation. On the other hand, if not only expectation but also knowledge and interpretation affect people's economic behavior, then changes in regimes itself may not be important in macroeconomics. A psychologist, Frederick Bartlett mentions that their existing organized pattern of knowledge about the world determines their interpretation of new information. If government understands and analyzes their existing organized pattern of knowledge about the world and provide new information which change its organizes pattern, then it might be successful for government to change their behavior. If the relationship between their existing organized pattern of knowledge about the world and new information determines a future movement of economic activities. then, this argument challenges the new classical economics and the rational expectations school which have emphasized the importance of expectation.[2]

On the other hand, if not only xpectation but also knowledge and interpretation affects people's economic behavior, then changes in regimes may not be important in macroeconomics.

J. M. Keynes says in the following way.

> Economic fluctuations are due to not only the instability due to speculation but also the instability due to the characteristics of human nature, Human nature represents a mathematical expectation, spontaneous optimism, animal spirits (a spontaneous urge to action rather than inaction) and pessimism. Expectation is replaced by both optimism and pessimism. This implies that economic boom is destined to end in a slump and economic slump is destined to end in economic boom.[3]

> If this is true, it is important for us to create economic system whose economic boom is not destined to end in a slump.[4]

J. M. Keynes analyzes the general theory and causes of unemployment in terms of effective demand, the marginal propensity to consume, the marginal efficiency of capital, incentives to liquidity and expectation. However, we are very critical of his analysis. Our view can be explained in the following diagram.

Surface structure
Deflation, economic depression.
Deep structure
Consumers enjoy lower prices for products.

If capitalists welcome cheaper labor, and consumers enjoy lower prices for products, which consumers made, then, this may bring about the increase in unemployment,

This psychological law says that there is a nonlinear relationship between reduction in income and degree in consumer's enjoyment of lower prices for products. This means that this degree becomes greater as a future expectation about reduction in income becomes high. It follows that the fact that consumers welcome lower prices leads to lower incomes. In other words, their lower incomes lead to the fact that they welcome lower prices. If they don't welcome lower prices even if their incomes decrease, then their incomes and unemployment do not decrease and therefore economic depression may not lead to great depression. If this is true, discretionary monetary and fiscal policy may not be effective with respect to output and employment. Effective economic policy is to increase people's real purchasing power in money by exchanging old currency with new currency and to establish Government enterprise which purchases economic goods when their prices are low.

Notes
(1) See John Maynard Keynes, *The General Theory of employment, interest and money,* Prometheus Books, 1997, p18.
(2) Frederick Bartlett, *The mind at work and play,* Allen and Unwin, 1951. *Thinking,* Allen and Unwin, 1958. *Remembering,* Cambridge University press, 1932.

See *The General Theory of Employment, interest and money,* pp.198-199.
(3) See *The General Theory of Employment, interest and money,* pp.161-162.
(4) See *The General Theory of Employment, interest and money,* pp.321-322.

"An eastern view criticizes discretionary macroeconomic policy, because a macroeconomic policy for economic recovery may lead to economic recession in the long run. The notion that all opposites are polar - that light and dark, winning and losing, good and evil are merely different aspects of the same phenomenon - is one of the basic principles of the Eastern way of life. Since all opposites are interdependent, their conflict can never result in the total victory of one side, but will always be a manifestation of the interplay between two sides.

In the East, a virtuous person is therefore not one who undertakes the impossible task of striving for the good and eliminating the bad, but rather one who is able to maintain a dynamic balance between good and bad. This notion of dynamic balance is essential to the way in which the unity of opposites is experienced in Eastern mysticism is never a static identity, but always a dynamic interplay between two extremes. This point has been emphasized most extensively by the Chinese sages in their symbolism of the archetypal poles yin and yang. They called the unity lying behind yin and yang the Tao and saw it as a process which brings about their interplay.

Suppose you have a ball going round a circle. If this movement is projected on to a screen, it becomes an oscillation between two extreme points. (To keep the analogy with Chinese thought, I have written Tao in the circle and have marked the extreme points of the oscillation with yin and yang).

The ball goes round the circle with constant speed, but in the projection it slows down as it reaches the edge, turn around, and then accelerate again only to slow down once more-and so on dynamic unity of polar opposites in endless cycles.

```
         YIN
          |
  ___     ↓
 /   \  -----|
|  TAO|      |
 \___/       |
             |
             |
            YANG
```

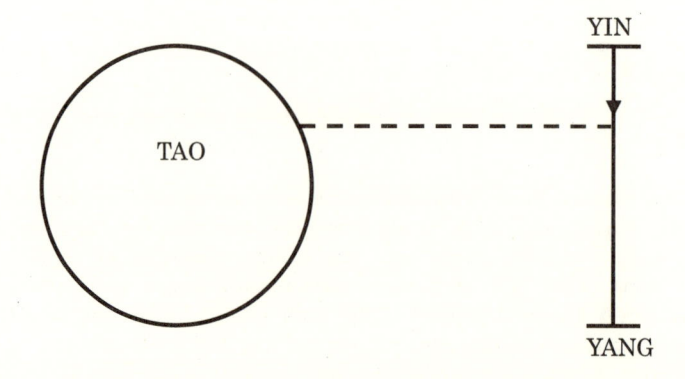

In any projection of that kind, the circular movement will appear an oscillation between two opposite points, but in the movement itself the opposites are unified and transcended. This image of a dynamic unification of opposites was indeed very much in the minds of the Chinese thinkers." (Fritjob Capra, *The Tao of physics an exploration of the parallels between modern physics and eastern mysticism,* Shambhala Publications, 2000, pp.146-147.)

Chapter2
J. M. Keynes's Treatise on Probability, New Classical Economics and Relevance Theory

Paul. M. Sweezy says in the following way.

> If, for example, the capitalists in the steel industry overestimate the demand for steel and produce more than the market can absorb at ruminative prices, they will contract their production and in so doing reduce the demand for labor power, iron, coal, transportation.
>
> There is no reason to suppose that there must take place a simultaneous expansion in the production of other commodities of such a nature as to make good the deficit in demand created by the cut in steel production.[1]

The arguments mentioned above implies that even if the capitalists have rational expectations, the capitalist system results in mistakes and confusion.

Kevin. D. Hoover says in the following ways.

> The existence of an empirically observed downward-sloping Phillips curve in Lucas's analysis depends crucially on the confusion by economic agents of absolute changes in the general level of prices with changes in relative prices, clearly, for agents with rational expectations, such confusion can result in random mistakes only. Mistakes can still be random, yet on average large or small. A rational agent would attempt to reduce the average size of his mistakes as much as possible. This means that he would attempt to as best he could to discern what fraction of any change in his

own price was actually a relative shift in his favor rather than pure inflation. In the language of engineering, he would try to extract the signal from the surrounding noise as efficiently as possible.[2]

The arguments mentioned above implies that economic agents based upon rational expectations can't forecast random mistakes.

If we analyze rational expectations in terms of relevance theory, economic agent's confusion results from the fact that old information and new information is random. As time goes on, new information becomes old information. After new information become old information, new information arises randomly.

New information may strengthen old information's assumption.

Or new information may weaken old information's assumption. The fact behind economic agent's confusion or random noise implies the interaction between old information and new information.

Rudolf Carnap says in the following way.

> Suppose the new evidence i is added to the prior evidence e for a hypothesis h. If the posterior confirmation c (h,e,i) is higher than the prior confirmation c (h,e), i is said to be positive to h on the evidence e, If it is lower, i is said to be negative.
>
> An observer x is interested in a hypothesis h, he possesses some prior evidence e and obtains now additional evidence i or considers the possibility of obtaining it. The chief question to be investigated is, how the c of h is influenced by the

addition of i to e.

If the posterior confirmation c (h,e,i) is higher than the prior confirmation c (h,e),we shall say that the additional evidence i is positively relevant or, simply, positive to the hypothesis h on the evidence e, If it is lower, we shall say that i is negatively relevant or negative to h one.

If the c of h remains unchanged, and also in another case, where c cannot be applied, we shall say that i is irrelevant to h one,

These relevance concepts was introduced and studied by W. E. Johnson and Keynes.[3]

Economic concepts of J. M. Keynes and new classical economics involves relevance theory. However, J. M. Keynes and rational expectation hypothesis ignore a context.

On the other hand, Speber and Wilson define relevance as a relation between an assumption and a context.

They define the concept of relevance in terms of economic principle and say in the following way.

> We want to compare the concept of relevance to concepts such as productivity or yield, which involve some form of cost-benefit analysis, a firm with output of any value, however small, is productive to some degree, just as we have claimed that an assumption with any contextual effects at all. however limited, is relevant to some degree.
>
> However, where the output is very small, there is some initial reluctance to say that the firm is productive at all. Even though, when compared to a firm with genuinely zero output, it is obviously productive to some degree, the parallel with relevance is clear. Similar remarks apply to the

assessment of relevance.

The contextual effects of an assumption in a given context are not the only factor to be taken into account in assessing its degree of relevance Contextual effects are brought about by mental processes. Mental processes, like all biological processes involve a certain effort, a certain expenditure of energy. The processing effort involved in achieving contextual effects is the second factor to be taken into account in assessing degrees of relevance. Processing effort is a negative factor Other things being equal, the greater the processing effort, the lower the relevance.[4]

J. M. Keynes and rational expectation hypothesis ignore the fact that the mistakes or errors people make depend upon their cognition, schema and knowledge or their own view of the world.

In other words, economics of Keynes and new classical economics ignore the fact that people try to interpret and understand new information or economic phenomena by their schema or their organized patterns of knowledge about economics or economic phenomena.

Notes
(1) Paul M Sweezy, *The theory of capitalist Development,* Monthly Review Press, 1942, p157.
(2) See Kevin D. Hoover, *the New classical macroeconomics* Basil Blackwell, 1988, p31.
(3) See R. Carnap, *Logical foundations of probability,* Routledge & Kegan Paul, 1950, pp.356-357.
(4) Dan Sperber and Deidre Wilson, *Relevance communication and cognition,* Blackwell, 1995.

Chapter 3
Expectation and Relevance Theory

What J. M. Keynes ignores in General Theory is schema, relevance theory and the interaction between old information and new information. What is common between Keynes's view in a treatise on probability, new classical economics and relevance theory is that the interaction between old information and new information affects people's decision to invest.[1]

Relevance theory tells us that the recovered financial position from a firm's debt position, monetary expenditure and a strong demand for the product of the firm stimulate and activate relevant expectations which lead to the increase in output, employment and prices.

The recovered financial position may be achieved by exchanging old currency with new currency whose value and purchasing power of money are higher than that of old currency.

Monetary expenditure is equivalent to public works a low interest rate and financial assistance to the poor.

A strong demand means that government enterprise purchases economic goods from a depressed firm, and creates new product which satisfy effectual demand. Hyman Minsky's financial instability hypothesis tells us that changes in expectation about future economic prospects causes the fluctuation in financial asset values and therefore the inescapable need for a government intervention may be essential

On the other hand, if we make a reinterpretation of the General Theory of Employment, Interest and Money, the need for a government intervention might imply changes in cognition, schema and people's interpretation of new information.

If this is true, the point is not government expenditures but changes in schema and cognition.

The reason is as follows. Capitalism is fundamentally flawed and an equilibrium system depends upon schema, cognition and people's interpretation of new information.

Hyman Minsky says in the following way.

> J. M. Keynes was interested in the process of decision-making under uncertainty, and his probability theory deals with various degrees of rational belief. He differentiates between the probability of a proposition and the weight attached to a proposition. As the relevant evidence increases, the magnitudes of the probability may either decrease or increase. Subjective probabilities assigned on the basis of insufficient knowledge are subject to quick and substantial changes. Economic decisions based upon such estimates can change both rapidly and markedly. In Keyne's view, in addition to the probability assigned to a conditional proposition either on objective or subjective grounds. There is another subjective factor which intervenes in decision-making. This is the weight or confidence with which the assigned probability is used as a guide to action or decision. In a treatise on probability, Keynes viewed an accretion of evidence as increasing the weight or confidence attached to a proposition. If economic decision - making under uncertainty is made on the basis of imperfect knowledge, and is central to the General Theory.[2]

It must be worthwhile analyzing The General Theory in terms of relevance theory. If investment is volatile because of economic decisions under imperfect knowledge and uncertainty, economy may reach to equilibrating tendencies as the relevant evidence increases.[3]

Relevance theory tells us that only monetary expenditure is not the remedy for economic recession, which derives from the effect of a collapse in financial market upon real economic variables because only monetary expenditure does not provide new evidence that a firm expect his profits to increase, if he makes new investment, increase output and employment. If we define relevant expectation as the state of confidence and optimism that makes a firm expect his profits to increase, then only monetary expenditure is not effective with respect to output and employment if people have relevant expectation.

Relevance theory tells us that only fiscal and monetary policy is not effective with respect to output and employment. Therefore it is important to create a new macroeconomic theory based upon relevance theory.[4]

Notes
(1) Bibography says that Relevance Theory by Dan Sperber and Deirdre Wilson is influenced by *Logical foundations of probability* by R. Carnap (1950) R. B. Braithwaite says that in the form of considering only propositions expressible in a language - system of an atomic character, this was the line taken by Rudolf Carnap, who elaborated a quasi - logical interpretation of probability using a formal apparatus of constructed language - systems.

Carnap related his interpretation to betting quotients and restrictions upon them, and this suggested to me the way of considering partial belief which I have just outlined. To treat the logic of partial belief as the theory of the rationality of betting quotients may seem a far cry from keynes's logical interpretation of probability. (*A treatise on probability : The*

collected writings of John Maynard Keynes, volume VIII, Macmillan, 1973. p.xxi
(2) Hyman P. Minsky, *John Maynard Keynes,* 2008 McGraw Hill pp.62-65.

(3) See A treatise on probability.
As the relevant evidence at our disposal increases, the magnitude of the probability of the argument may either decrease or increase, according as the new knowledge strengthens the unfavorable or the favorable evidence, but something seems to have increased in either case we have a more substantial basis upon which to rest our conclusion. I express this by saying that an accession of new evidence increases the weight of an argument. New evidence will sometimes decrease the probability of an argument, but it will always increase its 'weight'. If the new evidence is irrelevant, the weight is left unchanged. If any part of the new evidence is relevant, then the value is increased. The reason for our stricter definition of relevance is now apparent. If we are to be able to treat 'weight' and 'relevance' as correlative terms. We must regard evidence as relevant, part of which is favorable and part unfavorable, even if taken as a whole, it leaves the probability unchanged. With this definition, to say that a new piece of evidence is 'relevant' is the same thing as to say that it increases the 'weight' of the argument, In this case the weight of the argument is at it's lowest. Starting, therefore, with minimum weight, corresponding to a priori probability the evidential weight of an argument rises, though its probability may either rise or fall, with every accession of relevant evidence. (A treatise on probability, The collected writings of John Maynard Keynes, volume VIII, Macmillan, 1973, pp.77-78)

(4) First we need to understand what relevance means. Information is relevant to you if it interacts with your existing beliefs/thoughts (which Sperber and Wilson call assumptions). One product of this interaction is a contextual implication exemplified below. You wake up thinking 1) if it's raining, I won't go to the lecture this morning. You look out the window and discover 2) it's raining.
From existing assumption 1) and the new information 2), you can deduce further information 3) I won't go to the lecture this morning.
2) is relevant because, in the context of 1), it produces new information or contextually implies 3). Creating contextual implications is one kind of contextual effect - others are the strengthening or elimination of existing assumptions - and the greater the contextual effects the greater the

relevance.
The notion of relevance can be summed up in the following formulae.
....

7) Other things being equal the greater the contextual effects, the greater the relevance.

8) Other things being equal, the smaller the processing effort the greater the relevance.

An implicature is a contextual assumption or implication which a speaker, intending her utterance to be relevant, intended to make manifest to the hearer.

Let's look at an example to see how implications might operate in practice, consider the following exchange.

13) John: Would you drive a mercedes?
Mary: I wouldn't drive any expensive car.

14) A mercedes is an expensive car from which to derive the contextual implication.

15) Mary would not drive a mercedes. Mary's utterance and 14)here function as premises in an inferential syllogism to give the conclusion15).
(Andrew Goatly, *Language of metaphors,* Routledge, 1997, pp.137-140)

The linguistic idea behind relevance theory can be written down in the following way.

$X_t = Y_t - 1$
X = old information
Y = new information
Z = context
t = time
$X_t = a_1, a_2, a_3, a_4 , ...$
$Y_t = b_1, b_2, b_3, b_4 , ...$
$Z_t = c_1, c_2, c_3, c_4 , ...$
$X_t = Y_t\text{-}1$
$Z_t = f(x, y)$
$Y_t = f(x)$
G = the degree of relevance between X and Y
H = the degree of relevance between G and Z

As H becomes high, the possibility that people change their attitudes becomes high Relevance theory ignores people's weight. If we rewrite X in the following way.

$X_t = \theta_1 a_1 + \theta_2 a_2 + \theta_3 a_3 + \theta_4 a_4$ $\theta_1 + \theta_2 + \theta_3 + \theta_4 = 1$
If $\theta_1 = 1$, then $\theta_2 = 0$ $\theta_3 = 0$ $\theta_4 = 0$

With the addition of new information, the possibility that people change their attitudes depends upon the parameter of weight.

Chapter 4
A Multiplier Effect and a Fractal-based Economic System

Stuart Kauffman says in the following way.

A critical diversity of goods and services may be necessary for the sustained explosion of further technological diversity. Standard macroeconomic models ignore the growth of diversity of goods and services. Imagine that each year, certain kinds of symbol strings keep emerging out of the fertile soil of France. These symbol strings are the "renewable resources" of France, and might stand for grapes, wheat, coal, milk, iron, wood, wool, and so forth. There are the evolving technological possibilities open to France. At the first period, the French might consume all their renewable resources, Or they might consult the laws of technological complementarity engraved at the hotel de ville in each town and village, and consider all the possible new goods and services that might be created by using the renewable resources to "act" on one another, The iron might be made into forks, knives, and spoons, as well as axes. The milk might be made into ice cream.

The wheat and milk might be made into a porridge. Now at the next period, the French might consume what they had by way of renewable resources and the bounty of their first inventions or they might think about what else they could create.

Perhaps the ice cream and the grapes can be mixed. Or the ice cream and grapes mixed and placed in a baked shell made of wheat to create the first French pastry.

Perhaps the axe can be used as such to cut firewood.

Perhaps the wood and axe can be used as such to cut firewood. Perhaps the wood and axe can be used to create bridges across streams.[1]

What Stuart Kauffman emphasizes in the text of "At Home in the Universe" is the importance of technological frontier. This means that the goods and services previously "invented" create novel opportunities to create still more goods and services. Modern macroeconomics needs new economic models based upon technological convolution which means that economic diversity creates more economic diversity and economic growth. New economic models must involve the emergence of markets and behavior coordination among such agents.

In other words, new economic models involve the potential linkages between the diversity of economic sectors in economic growth. General Theory by J. M. Keynes and the multiplier effect ignores connections between various economic sectors and the relationship between economic diversification and economic growth. If government is successful in creating economic web which is mutually reinforcing, then it might create more economic wealth than just creating pyramid, roads, dams which does not create profits. The fact that economic diversity creates more economic diversity and this leads to a high economic growth corresponds to the law of increasing return by Alfred Marshall which means that an increase of numbers generally leads to a more than proportionate increase of collective efficiency. Afred Marshall says in the following way.

> An increase of capital and labor leads generally to an improved organization, and therefore in those industries which are not engaged in raising raw produce it generally gives a return increased more than in proportion, and further this improved organization tends to diminish or even override any increased resistance which nature may offer to raising increased amounts of raw produce,
>
> Taking account of the fact that an increasing density of population generally brings with it access to new social enjoyments and say - An increase of population accompanied by an equal increase in the material sources of enjoyment and aids to production is likely to lead to a more than proportionate increase in the aggregate income of enjoyment of all kinds.[2]

It is important to clarify the interrelationship between changes in policy regimes and changes in human behaviors.

The things in which J. M. Keynes, Milton Friedman T. J. Sargent and Robert Lucas are interested are quite the same in the sense that economics of Keynes. monetarism and new classical economics involve this interrelationship, If a change in policy regimes involves a change in human behaviors, then this may lead to a higher inflation, debt-deflation, unemployment and economic depression, However this also may contribute to a stable price, output, employment and economic prosperity.

General Theory by J. M. Keynes includes economic ideas of monetarist economy neoclassical economics and new classical economics, because J. M. Keynes fully recognizes the importance of market and expectation, the relation between changes in policy regimes and changes in human behavior. However, if discretionary economic policy is not effective with respect to output and employment, the reasons might be as follows. The first reason is that the multiplier effect does not depend upon the marginal propensity to consume.

The second reason is that a change in policy regime does not immediately lead to a change in human behaviors. The third reason is that the increase in investment or effective demand does not contribute to output and employment. If the hypothesis mentioned above is right, then the assumption which exists in General Theory must be corrected and modified. Otherwise, General Theory cannot contribute to employment, output and a price stability. What we should learn from economic policy of Yamada Houkoku is the importance of economic network and the fact that the causes of multiplier effect are the number of economic network. If this is true, the multiplier effect is minimal, provided that the number of economic network is minimal. If this hypothesis is true, government must create the increase in effectual demand and economic web in order to increase output and employment.

The effectiveness of a discretionary macroeconomic policy depends upon effectual demand and economic web.[3] The increase in effectual demand and economic web creates the effectiveness of multiplier, the increase in the number of exchange goods, and thus the increase in division of labor. If the extent of market is limited by effectual demand, then economic depression may be the fact that economic growth reaches to the limited extent of market, speculative money goes to the financial market and a collapse in economic bubbles occur. As long as economic bubbles create a collapse in stock markets, economic policy for economic recovery creates economic depression in the long run, not in the short run. If we follow the hypothesis mentioned above, the important thing for economic recovery is to create and find out effectual demand or expand and increase the limited extent of market. The following mathematical equation may explain the relationship between interaction and multiplier.

1+1+1+1+1=5······(1)

1+1+1+1+1=1······(2)

The mathematical equation (1) and the mathematical equation (2) are quite different in the sense that the result derived from the equation (1) is higher than the result from the equation (2). In the equation (1) interaction does work. However, in the equation (2) interaction does not work. The above analysis tells us that even if Government spend the same amount of expenditures, the multiplier effect in the economic structure (1) is larger than the one in the economic structure (2).

If we have five economic elements and economic interaction is positive, the adding up of five economic elements leads to more than five such as fifteen according to the effect of interaction or the multiplier effect.

On the other hand, the adding up of five economic elements may lead to less than five because of negative interaction or negative multiplier. Even if Government intervenes in the market, this only leads to a huge government deficit or a higher inflation which has no effect upon output and employment because of negative interaction. Economic structure (1) and economic structure (2) seems to be quite the same on the surface structure level. However, economic structure (1) and economic structure (2) are quite different on the deep structure level.

If we clarify real economic structure behind the economic structure (1) and economic structure (2), then the following structure can be written down.

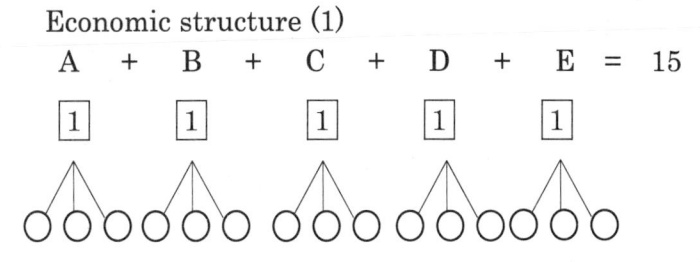

Economic structure (1)

A + B + C + D + E = 15

$\boxed{1}$ $\boxed{1}$ $\boxed{1}$ $\boxed{1}$ $\boxed{1}$

△△ △△ △△ △△ △△
○○○ ○○○ ○○○ ○○○ ○○○

Each economic element (A, B, C, D, E) controls three.

Economic structure (2)

A + B + C + D + E = 5

$\boxed{1}$ $\boxed{1}$ $\boxed{1}$ $\boxed{1}$ $\boxed{1}$
↓   ↓   ↓   ↓   ↓
(negative) (negative) (negative) (negative) (negative)

Each economic element (A, B, C, D, E) does not control three economic elements and the effect of each interaction is negative.

The above equation tells us that an invisible hand argued by Adam Smith in the Wealth of Nations implies the positive interaction, not competitive efficiency. Economic network which is not based upon competition and efficiency may increase the multiplier effect argued by John Maynard Keynes in General Theory.

If company A, company B, company C, company D compete each other in order for only one company, to maixmize his profits, they tend to reduce the prices of their products In other words, price competition occurs, which leads to deflation and the reduced wage rates. On the other hand, if Government encourages economic network based upon a fractal economic system to emerge, then an economic coordination between them may lead to inflation, and the increased wage rates.

An economic coordination can be explained in the following way.

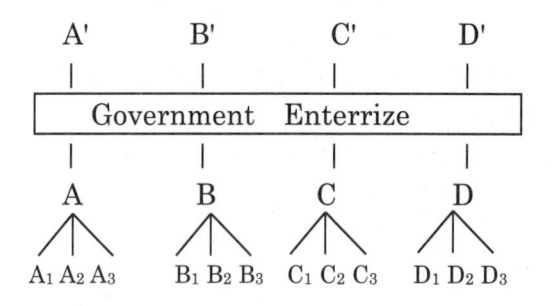

```
    A'        B'        C'        D'
    |         |         |         |
   ┌─────────────────────────────────┐
   │   Government    Enterrize       │
   └─────────────────────────────────┘
    |         |         |         |
    A         B         C         D
   /|\       /|\       /|\       /|\
  A₁ A₂ A₃  B₁ B₂ B₃  C₁ C₂ C₃  D₁ D₂ D₃
```

Government enterprise purchases economic goods from A, B, C and D and creates new economic goods, A' B' C' D'. If their economic goods corresponds to effectual demand, then

A_1, A_2, A_3, B_1, B_2, B_3, C_1, C_2, C_3, D_1, D_2, D_3, A, B, C, D and government enterprise are in the same boat and the same company. This means that economic network based upon a fractal economic system, does not lead to economic competition and encourage each company to increase output and employment.

Each company and government enterprise are on an equal basis, because each company is interdependent each other and each economic goods each company produces does not exist without economic goods which other company produces.

Other company's goods are indispensable for each company and therefore a fractal economic system represents economic complementary relationship. A fractal based economic system can be explained by the concept of Deep structure argued by Noam Chomsky.[4]

J. M. Keynes says that a monetary economy is one in which changing views about the future economy are capable of influencing the quantity of employment,

If this is true, we are thus led to a more general theory which explains how a monetary economy which changing views about the future does not influence the quantity of employment. If changing views about the future, the effect of money and financial fluctuations have a minimum effect upon real economy, we could maintain a healthy economy and avoid a depressed economy. If changing views about the future, the effect of money and financial fluctuations reduce the number of exchange of goods and production processes, then logic tells us that economic recovery is to minimize the effect of changing views about the future, and the effect of money and financial fluctuations upon real economy. If economic structure is based upon a fractal based economic network, this may lessen and minimize the effect of changes in the value of money upon real economy. This implies that Government should create economic organization which stimulates exchange of goods.

In other words, if Government creates effectual demand and a new product which maximizes the number and amount of exchange of goods, then the new product does not create a creative destruction. A creative creation which means that the new product C is created by the interaction between the product B and the product A. A creative destruction means that the increase in the production of C leads to the decrease in the production of B or A. If the new product D satisfy effectual demand, and is created by the interaction between C, B and A, then the new product D contributes to the increase in employment. The definition of effectual demand implies that Say's Law holds and supply creates demand. J. M. Keynes' General Theory emphasizes that expectation determines employment. However, economic principle and principle of uncertainty tells us that great depression makes the situation that expectation does not determine employment, because it stimulates economic principle, which emerges a firm to reduce the amount of employment. On the other hand, economic boom may make the situation that expectation determines employment. Uncertainty about the future and risk for loss discourage a firm to increase the amount of employment.

However, if uncertainty about the future and risk for loss is low, then a firm may increase output and employment. Government enterprise and a fractal-based economic system reduce uncertainty about the future because people believe that the products manufactured by them would be sold out. A fractal economic network is based upon credit and certainty. This means that a fractal economic network does not function well if each private company have any doubt that government enterprise might not purchase their economic goods. Adam Smith gives us the following economic argument.

(1) Division of labour is the great cause of its increased power.

(2) Division of labour arises from a propensity in human

nature to exchange.

(3) Division of labour is limited by the extent of the power of exchange.

(4) Difficulties of barter lead to the selection of one commodity as money.

If this is true, division of labour leads to employment. An increase in economic web and economic network lead to division of labour and employment.[5] If division of labour is limited by the extent of the power of exchange, then the solution for economic recovery is for government to create, expand market, and increase people's power of exchange.

A fractal based economic network creates a multiplied increase in the number of division of labor and employment As we mentioned earlier difficulties of barter lead to the selection of one commodity as money.

However the selection of money as the means of exchange may lead to a fluctuation in the value of money which may lead to the decrease in exchange of goods and thus output or employment. If this is true, economic recovery implies the decrease in difficulties of barter. The difficulties of barter may lead to the decrease in the amount of exchange. However, if economic structure is based upon a fractal based economic network, this lessen or minimize the effect of changes in the value of money upon real economy and increases the amount of exchange.

Alfred Marshall says in the following way.

> The most important of these result from the growth of correlated branches of industry which mutually assist one another, perhaps being concentrated in the same localities, but anyhow availing themselves of the modern facilities for

communication offered by steam transport, by the telegraph and by the printing press.[6]

A fractal-based economic system implies the growth of correlated branches of industry which mutually assist one another. Therefore, this system prevents economic crises arising from disproportionality from occurring. If disproportionality is one of the real causes of economic crises as Karl Marx suggests, then economic crises never occur, as long as production is correctly proportional to the various branches of industry. A fractal-based economic system inplies the fact that production is correctly proportional to the various branches of industry.

There is the argument to support the construction of a fractal-based economic system in the following way.

> Snow in the Hindu Kush mountains gives water to the land of Afghanistan, but there has been less and less snow year after year.
> Dr. Nakamura was afraid that a serious drought might hit the area again and that the wells would not be able to supply enough water for both drinking and farming.
> His next plan was to make a canal which would be connected to the Kunar River, a French branch of the Indus River.[7]

The argument mentioned above provides to us the intuitive idea that we should construct a fractal-based economic system whose a private firm is connected with government enterprises which is connected to effectual demand. A nonlinear relationship between the increase in income and the increase in marginal propensity to consume in a wealthy community is inherent in a capitalist economy. Therefore the point is that we should change a capitalist economy into a new economic system which is inherent in a proportionality between the increase in income and the increase in marginal propensity to consume.

Notes
(1) See Stuart Kauffman, *At Home in,* the Universe Oxford University Press 1995, p289
(2) See Alfred Marshall, *Principles of economics,* vol.1, Macmillan and Co., 1890, p.374.

(3) See The Wealth of Nations.
    The actual price at which any commodity is commonly sold is called its market price. It may either be above or below, or exactly the same with its natural price. The market price of every particular commodity is regulated by the proportion between the quantity which is actually brought to market, and the demand of those who are willing to pay the natural price of the commodity or the whole value of the rent, labour, and profit, which must be paid in order to bring it thither. Such people may be called the effectual demanders, and their demand the effectual demand: since it may be sufficient to effectuate the bringing of the commodity to market. It is different from the absolute demand, A very poor man may be said in same sense to have a demand for a coach and six, he might like to have it, but his demand is not an effectual demand, as the commodity can never be brought to market in order to satisfy it. When the quantity of any commodity which is brought to market falls short of the effectual demand, all those who are willing to pay the whole value of the rent, wages, and profit, which must be paid in order to bring it thither, cannot be supplied with the quantity which they want, When the quantity brought falls short of the effectual demand, the market price rises above the natural When it exceeds the effectual demand the market price falls below the natural. When the quantity brought to market is just sufficient to supply the effectual demand and no more, the market price naturally comes to be either exactly or as nearly as can be judged the same with the natural price. The quantity never should exceed

the effectual demand.(Adam Smith *The Wealth of Nations,* Bantam Classic, 2003, pp.79-82)

(4) Noam Chomsky, *Aspects of the theory of syntax* MIT press, 1965, pp.128-147.
(5) Adam Smith says that the division of labour is limited by the extent of the market. (Adam Smith, *The Wealth of Nations,* Bantam Classic, 2003, p.27)
(6) Alfred Marshall, *Principles of economics,* vol.1, Macmillan and Co.,1890, pp.376.
(7) See *Living together Pro-vision,* English Course I Lesson 10, Kirihara Shoten, 2010.

Chapter5
Generative Economics, Current Macroeconomics and Communication

New classical economics criticizes Keynesian macroeconomics, not J. M. Keynes's General Theory because Keynesian macroeconomics is based upon a structure stability and invariant parameters. If identifying a structural model is wrong, then it is important for economists to clarify J. M. Keynes's thoughts and analyze the General Theory in terms of the creative aspect. Rational expectations hypothesis says that people understand economic laws of motion. This models people as making decisions in dynamic settings in the faced well-defined constraints Thomas J. Sargent says that people's behavior patterns will vary systematically with changes in government policies or the rules of the game well-defined constraints include laws of motion over time that describe such thing as the taxes that people must pay and the prices of the goods that they buy and sell.[1]

Rational expectations hypothesis emphasizes that people understand economic laws of motion and therefore people's behavior will change when they are confronted with changes in economic policy.

However cognitive linguistics, relevance theory and generative grammar challenges rational expectations hypothesis because they emphasizes the fact that schema, cognition, relevance, a creative aspect of human nature, deep structure, and people's existing pattern of knowledge determine people's behavior. The fact that a change in policy rules changes agent's expectations of future policy actions involves interpretative work, people's understanding of new information and a change in policy regimes depends upon the processes and principles involved in the interplay between knowledge of economic system knowledge of context and situation and background schematic knowledge New classical economics assumes that people have limited information, receive information about some prices more often than other prices, and make a decision on the basis of their limited information.[2] However this assumption is inconsistent with the arguments of linguistics.

Rational expectations hypothesis does not clarify the mechanism that laws of motion change over time.

If we apply concept of metaphor to the analysis of rational expectations hypothesis, laws of motion vary, depending upon people's background and schematic knowledge. Andrew Goatly says in the following way.

> The metaphors we use structure our thinking, hiding some features of the phenomena we apply them to, and highlighting others, If, for example. I use chess as a metaphor for a battle, it will highlight features of the battle like casualties, relative power and mobility of fighters and positions of forces.[3]

If the metaphors we use structure our thinking, then changing people's metaphors may lead to the effectiveness of discretionary macro economic policy. Rational expectations hypothesis says that tighter money now can mean higher inflation now.[4]

One argument about the one mentioned above is that this argument should be understood as a response or something

Another argument is that this argument should be understood as a creative process learned through reinforcement. Noam Chomsky says in the following way.

> Within traditional linguistic theory, furthermore, it was clearly understood that one of the qualities that all languages have in common is their "creative" aspect. Thus an essential property of language is that it provides the means for expressing indefinitely many thoughts and for reacting appropriately in an indefinite range of new situations. The grammar of a particular language then is to be supplemented by a universal grammar that accommodates the creative aspect of language use and expresses the deep-seated regularities which being universal, are omitted from the grammar itself. Modern linguistics has not attempted to deal with the creative aspect of language use. It thus suggests no way to overcome the fundamental descriptive inadequacy of structuralist grammars. Another reason for the failure of traditional grammars, particular or universal, to attempt a premise statement of regular processes of sentence formation.[5]

Noam Chomsky criticizes a traditional linguistic concept, emphacture and surface structure. Noam Chomsky criticizes the structuralists' contention that linguists should describe sentences and not speculate about the psychology of those who produce the sentences. [6]

Also he emphasizes the importance of deep syntactical structure and says that an invisible God created the visible world.[7]

A central idea in much of current macroeconomic is that

this should be studied independently of our thinking.[8]

However, economics is a branch of psychology, cognitive sciences, and linguistics.

Economic phenomena can be derived from deep structure of economic structure, people's mind, not surface structure such as a corpus of economic data.

He criticizes empiricism and supports the rationalist approach.

The organization of a generative grammar says that knowledge of a language involves the implicit ability to understand indefinitely many sentences and therefore a generative grammar must be a system of rules that can iterate to generate an indefinitely large number of structures.[9]

Current macroeconomics does not analyze the intrinsic cognitive capacities of an organism and the system of belief and behavior.

Noam Chomsky criticizes behaviorism and explaines in the following way.

> When Skinner's theories deriving from his painstaking experiments in conditioning rats and pigeons are literally interpreted, they are clearly inapplicable to most human behavior, If one takes a food pellet as "positive reinforce" and provides lever depressing as operant behavior, one can get some substantial notion of how rats may be conditioned by their environment. Positive reinforcement can be stretched to cover not only food, money, sex and so on but also intellectual explanations. If we take the very elementary human software capacity of generating the sentences of a particular language (a capacity that comes to the force

universally with little or no explicit training), we then have an "infinite response" capacity that could never derive from reinforcement of specified behavior. By the same token, the skinnerian notion that all our behavior is essentially a response, which amounts to a kind of statistical determinism is shown not to apply to our linguistic software. When put to the test of generating a grammatical sentence, a human being so far as his basic linguistic capacity goes, has an infinite number of possible responses available. Since, as has been made clear, this means that no significant probability of occurrence can be assigned to the production of grammatical sentences, as opposed to ungrammatical sentences. What is produced is likely to be entirely new behaviour. It follows that such behavior cannot be understood as a response, or something "learned" through "reinforcement". at all. Producing a grammatical sentence is not a deterministic activity at all, Internalized generative software produces a grammatical sentence. [10]

The same logic can be applied to economic analysis.

A central idea in much of current macroeconomic is that this should be studied independently of the fact that an invisible God created the visible world.

Macroeconometric models seem to argue that a corpus of data matters and should not speculate about human psychology.

Macroeconometric models is concerned with what people are doing and not with what people think.

However, Generative grammar by Noam Chomsky tells us that macroeconomics should not be concerned only with what is observable and observed human behavior. It may also tells us that macroeconomics should deal with subjective thoughts and feelings.

Current macroeconomics would argue that people's judgments about what they are doing are in principle essentially irrelevant.

Economic data, its description and econometric analysis does not clarify people's generative device.

Econometric analysis and a mathematical macroeconomic model insists on just considering noise, not the generating source of the noise. The rational expectations school or new classical economics challenged the traditional Keynesian models. However, not only new classical economics and the traditional Keynesian models but even J. M. Keynes's General Theory seems to understand new economic behavior as a response or something "learned" through "reinforcement".

On the other hand, new economic behavior can be explained by an invisible deep structure or generative devices within human psychology.

Our hypothesis of economic generative devices is that it includes economic principle, relevance, concept of metaphor, schema, mental framework.

In other words, it involves knowledge of new situation, and background schematic knowledge.[11]

Economic generative device may involve relevance and the process of communication. The effect of macroeconomic policy upon people's behavior must be considered in terms of illocutionary force perlocutionary effect and inference. Economics is concerned with the inferential principles and economic generative device may provide a coherent explanation of people's interpretation of new information and a change in policy regimes. If we create new economics based upon linguistics and define it as generative economics, it may challenge new classical economics and revives a discretionary macroeconomic policy.[12]

Notes
(1) Preston J. Miller (ed), *The Rational Expectations Revolution Reading from the Front Line*, the MIT press, p.33.
(2) Preston J. Miller (ed), *The Rational Expectations Revolution Reading from the Front Line*, the MIT press, p.17.
(3) Anderw Goatly, *The Language of metaphors,* Routledge, 1997, p.2.
(4) Preston J. Miller (ed), *The Rational Expectations Revolution Reading from the Front Line*, the MIT press, p.109.
(5) Aspects of the theory of syntax by Noam Chomsky MIT press, 1965, pp.3-8
(6) Justin Leifer, *Noam Chomsky : a philosophic Overview,* Twayne publishers, 1975.
(7) Justin Leifer, *Noam Chomsky : a philosophic Overview,* Twayne publishers, 1975, p.132.
(8) George Soros says in the following way "The concept of open society is based on the recognition that our understanding of the world is inherently imperfect" George Soros, *Open society, Reforming Global capitalism,* 2000, p.3)
"Natural scientists think about a universe that is independent of their thinking" (George Soros, *Open society Reforming Global capitalism,* p.9)
(9) Noam Chomsky, *Aspects of the theory of syntax,* the MIT press, pp.15-16.
(10) Justin Leifer. *Noam Chomsky : a philosophic Overview,* Twayne publishers, pp.141-143.
(11) Anderw Goatly, *The Language of metaphors,* Routledge, 1997, pp.137-139.
(12) When we consider, and analyze communication, we could not ignore the concept of illocutionary force and perlocutionary effect, these are explained in the following way.

> "An utterance has a certain illocution and make people change their behaviours Pragmatic possibilities are not signaled in the language itself and instead inferred from the context in which the utterance is made. Perlocutionary effect means some kind of effect on the second person given by an utterance such as frighten, persuade" (H. G. Widdowson, *Linguistics,* Oxford University Press, 1996, pp.62-63.)

Relevance theory tells us that people may ignore all information which is irrelevant to context. H. G. Widdowson gives us the following example which is related with context and schema.

"When people make an indexical connection, they do so by linking features of the language with familiar features of their world, with what is established in their minds as a normal pattern of reality or schema. In other words, content is a schematic construct. The achievement of pragmatic meaning is a matter of matching up the linguistic elements of the code with the schematic elements of the context. So, for example, if you were to hear someone make the remark 'Brazil scored just before the final whistle', the likelihood is that the word 'Brazil' would not call to mind the Amazonian rain forests, coffee, or Copacabana Beach (schematic associations which might be relevant on other contextual occasions), but a football team celebrated for its skill."

The football schema thus engaged would lead you to infer what the expressions 'scored' and 'final whistle' referred to among all the possibilities that they might refer to in other contexts.

Reference is achieved when both speaker and hearer engage the same context by converging on what is schematically relevant. The same thing applies to the achievement of force. The utterance, it was suggested, could be taken as a warming. How might such a force be inferred? Again, the notion of schema comes in, people in a particular community have common assumptions not only about the way the world is organized, but also about the customary ways that social actions like speech acts are performed.(H. G. Widdowson, *Linguistics,* Oxford University Press, 1996, pp.63-64)

References

Adam Smith, *The wealth of Nations,* Bantam Classic, 2003.
Andrew Goatly, *The Language of metaphors,* Routledge, 1997.
Alfred Marshall, *Principles of economics,* vol.1, Macmillan and Co., 1890.
Ancrew Goatly, *The Language of metaphors,* Routledge, 1997.
R. Carnap, *Logical foundations of probafility,* Routledge & Kegon Paul London 1950.
Dan Sperber and Deirdre Wilson, *Relevance, Communication and Cognition,* (Second edition) Blackwell Publishing, 1995.
Fritjof Capra, *Tao of physics an exploration of the parallels between modern physics and eastern mysticism,* Shambhala Publications, 2000.
John Maynard Keynes, *Essays in Persuaion,* Macmillan and Co. Limited, 1931.
John Maynard Keynes, *The general theory of employment, interest and money,* Prometheus Books, 1997.
John Maynard Keynes, *A treatise on probability : The collected writings of John Maynard Keynes,* volume Ⅷ, Macmillan, 1973.
Karl Marx, *Capital,* volume 1,2,3, Foreign Language Publishing House, 1958.
Kevin D. Hoover, *The new classical macroeconomics,* Basil Blackwell, 1988.
Justin Leifer, *Noam Chomsky : a philosophic Overview,* Twayne publishers, 1975.
Hyman P. Minsky, *John Maynard Keynes,* McGraw Hill, 2008.
George Soros, *Open society : Reforming Global Capitalism,* Little, Brown and Company, 2000.
Noam Chomsky, *Aspects of the theory of syntax,* MIT press, 1965.
Preston J. Miller. *The rational expectations revolution readings from the Front Line,* MIT press, 1994.
Paul M. Sweezy, *the theory of capitalist development monthly,* Review Press, 1942.
Stuart Kauffman, *At Home in the Universe,* Oxford University Press, 1955.
Rouald W. Langacker, *Foundations of Cognitive Grammar,* volume 1, theoretical prerequisites, Stanford University Press, 1987.

Short notes on the real causes of economic depression

Unlike Milton Friedman and J. M. Keynes, the implication which economic policy of Yamada Houkoku gives us is as follows. The real causes of economic depression is a collapse in a multilateral payment system, which is due to a changing economic structure, not a short supply of money, on an insufficient effective demand.

In the nineteenth century. Britain had a trade deficit, but she had a current account surplus.[1]

This contributed to growth of world economy and a development in a multilateral payment system.

If this is true, fiscal policy and public expenditures would not increase the multiplier effect upon economy.

In other words, the effect of fiscal policy and the multiplier effect may depend upon economic diversity economic network and economic web. It follows that economic policy for solving economic depression is to increase economic diversity.

If financial crisis is due to a collapse in a multilateral payment system, and an imbalance between saving and investment, then a saving money would go to a financial market, which may result in economic bubble.

Economic bubble would lead to a collapse in economic bubble and a reduction in real purchasing power in money.[2]

An increase in money or huge government expenditure does contribute little to economic recovery.

Economic diversity means that different companies produce different products. In other words, an increase in economic diversity leads to the stability of prices, not price competition. This means that a decrease in economic diversity leads to price competition or deflation. Deflation may be just a decrease in economic diversity which is due to a collapse in a multilateral payment system.

Inflation may be just an increase in economic diversity which is due to a development in a multilateral payment system.

If this is true, the purpose of government intervention is to increase economic diversity, create a multilateral payment system and expand economic web.

If the imbalance between saving and investment is due to a decrease in economic diversity, and a collapse in a multilateral payment system, then inflation, deflation and fluctuations in asset prices is just a natural phenomenon which arises out of economic web and an interrelationship between economic branches within a country. The above argument says that the stability of prices or financial stability depends upon the stability of economic web, a multilateral payment system and a proportional growth in different economic branches. The amount of investment and employment and the degree of financial stability are limited by the number of economic network. A purchasing power in money is a natural phenomenon which arises out of the degree of stability of a multilateral payment system.

Notes
(1) See S. B. Saul, *Studies in British Overseas Trade, 1870-1914,* Liverpool University Press, 1960.
(2) With respect to an imbalance between saving and investment, see *The collected writings of John Maynard Keynes,* volume xxv activities 1940-1944 shaping the post-war world the clearing union, the Macmillan Press, 1980.

Supplement: a Proposal for the Establishment of "International Buikukyoku"

In my view, one of the causes of financial crisis and economic depression is the fact that key currencies such as yen, pond and dollar are available all over the world.

This fact may lead to capital mobility hot money and financial speculation.

In other words, financial crisis is purely a phenomenon that a domestic currency is exchangeable with a foreign currency.

Another reason for financial crisis is the fact that economic web or economic network always changes according to the changes in demand.

In other words, money goes to financial assets, not economic goods, with the changes in demand.

This means that the current economic web or network does not satisfy the changes in demand.

If this is true, the creation of new economic network, which satisfy the changes in demand, prevents money from going to financial assets.

The establishment of "International Buikukyoku" is necessary for us to prevent financial crisis and economic depression from occurring.

The purpose of this organization is to lend different economic areas the new paper currency and recommend them to produce economic goods which will be promised to be bought back by him. He is also intended to create new economic web. If we analyze inflation or deflation in terms of human perception or human cognition then deflation may be the degree of uncertainty or belief that the prices of economic goods may be too high for consumers to purchase.

The same argument can be applied to the analysis of inflation.

Inflation may be the degree of uncertainty or belief that the price of economic goods may not be too high for consumers to purchase.

The similar argument can be found in the analysis of investment and economic fluctuations.

Uncertainty that investment may lead to overproduction may contribute to unemployment and economic depression.

If this is true, economic recovery means increasing the degree of certainty.

In other words, certainty or their beliefs must lead to inflation or recovery from deflation, that the prices of economic goods may not be too high for consumers to purchase.

An interaction between government enterprise and private enterprise will create certainty, new demand and economic web. Economic idea behind optimal currency area is based upon the assumption of " free trade of goods" and "free mobility of people. "However, optimal currency area must be based upon the assumption of " a fractal-based economic network".

New economic web will increase certainty and decrease risks of investment.

Local branch of "International Buikukyoku" will be successful in creating new economic web and complementary goods which contribute to stimulate demand for private enterprise.

If new local paper currency, which corresponds to " Hansatsu in Edo period" is available only within local economic areas and accepted, then this will contribute to the stability of financial market.

Like a broach which complements a lady's dress a Government enterprise complements a private enterprise.

A conflict between a government enterprise based upon non-economic principle and a private enterprise based upon an economic principle creates new demand and economic prosperity,

For example, overproduction of a lady's dress creates new demand and new innovation because a government enterprise creates a broach. By creating a government enterprise which creates complementary goods, overproduction of a private enterprise which is in conflict with a government enterprise will create new demand and new innovation.

The purpose of government enterprise is to create complementary goods and to reduce unemployment.

Even if private enterprise creates quite the same goods, new innovation and new demand occurs, provided that government enterprise creates complementary goods.

In other words, an international price competition and deflation never occur, with the complementary relation between government enterprise and private enterprise.

In J. M. keynes's view, the amount of employment depends upon effective demand.

In Yamada Houkoku's view, the amount of employment depends upon the number of division of labor, the number of innovation and the extent of economic diversity.

The complementary relationship between government enterprise and private enterprises creates a number of division of labor, a number of innovation and an increased economic diversity. The normal fluctuation of financial market does not change, even if external shocks occur, as long as economic web satisfy the changes in demand. In other words, economic prosperity does not change into economic depression, provided that economic network continues to create new demand and new innovation.

Economy moves independently even if external shocks occurs as long as economic web continues to create new economic relationship between complements and substitutes.[1]

In other words, external shocks do not create economic fluctuations if economy follows its own path.

If government enterprise is successful in increasing the number of potential complement or substitute relation, this means that economic diversity and economic web achieve local economic growth.

Western concept of conflict and contradiction can be found in Karl Marx's "Capital" and J. M. Keynes's "General Theory"

However, the notion of complementarity in the Eastern tradition is quite different from western concept and contradiction in the sense that conflict and contradiction create growth and harmony.[2] If this is true, the establishment of government enterprise which is in conflict with private enterprise will create economic growth new demand and economic diversity.

If economic depression is due to the fact that economic relation between complements and substitutes changes because of the change in demand, external shocks and innovation, then economic policy must be intended to achieve new economic relationship, and maximize the number of complements and substitutes, not huge government expenditures, If conflict and contradiction create growth and harmony economic policy for economic recovery must be to create the opposites which are complementary.

Under a centrally-planned economy, economic policy for economic recovery must be to create a private enterprise which is complementary,

On the other hand, under a capitalist economy the policy for economic recovery must be to create a government enterprise which is complementary.

Note
(1) More generally we need to consider "complements" and "substitutes". Screw and screw driver are complements, screw and nail are substitutes, Complements must be used together to create value Substitutes replace one another. Rather obviously, the complements, and substitutes of any good or service constitute the economic niche in which that good or service lives. An economic web is just the set of goods and services in an economy, linked by red lines between substitutes and green lines between complements. The more objects there are in the economy, the more complement and substitute relations exist among those objects as well as potential new objects in the adjacent possible.

As the diversity of the objects in the web increases, the diversity of prospective niches for new goods and services increase even more rapidly.

The very diversity of the economic web is autocatalytic. If this view is correct, then diversity of goods and services is a major driver of economic growth. Jone Jacobs emphasizes the relation between economic growth and economic diversity of cities. Jose Scheinkman found that economic growth correlated with economic diversity in the city. In a similar spirit, microfinancing of a liked diversity of cottage businesses in the third world and the first world seems to be achieving local economic growth where more massive efforts at education and infrastructure. Aswan dams and power grids seem to fail. Indeed, in the same way in an ecosystem, organisms create niches for other organisms. The Wright brothers airplane was a recombination between an airfoil, a light gasoline engine, bicycle wheels and a propeller, The more objects an economy has the more novel objects be constructed.

(Stuart A. Kauffman, *Investigations*, Oxford University Press, 2000, pp.226-229)

(2) Niels Bohr has introduced the notion of complementary. He considered the particle picture and the wave picture as two complementary descriptions of the same reality, each of them being only partly correct and having a limited range of application.

Each picture is needed to give a full description of the atomic reality and both are to be applied with in the limitations given by the uncertainty principle. This notion of complementarity has become an essential part of the way physicists think about nature and Bohr has often suggested that, it might be a useful concept also outside the field of physics. In fact the notion of complementarity proved to be extremely useful 2,500 years ago. It played an essential role in ancient Chinese thought which was based on the insight that opposite concepts stand in a polar - or complementary - relationship to each other.

The Chinese sages represented this complementarity of opposites by the archetypal polls yin and yang and saw their dynamic interplay as the essence of all natural phenomena and all human situations. (Fritjof Capra, *The Tao of physics an exploration of the parallels between modern physics and eastern mysticism,* Shambhala, 2000, p.160)

■ Author

Yasuhisa Miyake

　　Yasuhisa Miyake lived in the apartment where J. M. Keynes had lived in London, while studied economics at University of London and was born on February 21 when Yamada Houkoku was born.

　　He is currently a founding general-secretary of Yamada Houkoku Research Association.

502, Koyama, Okayama City, Okayama Prefecture Japan
701-1352
E-mail:houkoku0221m.jp@gmail.com

Cognition, Macroeconomics and Economic Policy of Yamada Houkoku

2012年10月20日　初版第1刷発行

■著　　　者────三宅康久
■発 行 者────佐藤　守
■発 行 所────株式会社 **大学教育出版**
　　　　　　　　〒700-0953　岡山市南区西市855-4
　　　　　　　　電話 (086)244-1268㈹　FAX (086)246-0294
■印刷製本────サンコー印刷㈱

Ⓒ Yasuhisa Miyake 2012, Printed in Japan
検印省略　　落丁・乱丁本はお取り替えいたします。
無断で本書の一部または全部を複写・複製することは禁じられています。

ISBN978 - 4 - 86429 - 164 - 4